To Julie —
Love and happiness along
your journey!
Michael

THE INSIDE-OUT EFFECT

A PRACTICAL GUIDE TO TRANSFORMATIONAL LEADERSHIP

BEHNAM TABRIZI | MICHAEL TERRELL

"THE INSIDE-OUT EFFECT: A Practical Guide to Transformational Leadership"

Published by Evolve Publishing, Inc.
www.evolvepublishing.com

Cover design by Kirk DouPonce inspired by the original cover concept of Avantika Agarwal.
Photograph of Behnam Tabrizi by dePolo Photography.
Photograph of Michael Terrell by Sam Shapiro.

978-0-9882245-9-9 hardcover
978-0-9882245-2-0 ePUB
978-0-9882245-3-7 ePDF

Printed in the United States of America

10 9 8 7 6 5 4 3 2 1

YOUR NAME: _____

What are three of your truest core values?
(Give yourself a minute or two to think.)

    1. _____

    2. _____

    3. _____

The book you are about to read is not your everyday book. Its pages are designed to be written in, creased, and, on occasion, ripped right out. There is nothing clean and tidy about embarking on transformation and the pages that follow are a reflection of that. Think of this book as a map and as a toolkit. Maps often have to be folded, reoriented, and traced on. Tools have to be used. The good news is by filling out this first page, you've already taken the first step! Keep it up. Keep your pen close as we push forward. To get the most out of this journey, prepare to make it yours.

Note: If you prefer to do most of your work on a computer, many of the tools and exercises in this book can be found on our website, www.theinsideouteffect.com

"What lies behind you and what lies in front of you pales in comparison to what lies within you."

—RALPH WALDO EMERSON

BEHNAM:

To my uncle and mentor, Firooz Tabrizi, MD,
who encouraged me to write this book,

and

my daughter and hero, Sheila Tabrizi,
and her generation who give me hope.

MICHAEL:

To my mom, Ann, who taught me
the meaning of leadership,

and

my dad, Glenn, who showed me
that lasting change starts within.

CONTENTS

STEP THREE
LEAD: AM I AUTHENTICALLY LEADING OTHERS?

THE ROAD AHEAD

CONTENTS

PREFACE

For the majority of our careers, the two of us have dedicated ourselves to helping others transform their lives. It's our passion. It's what invigorates us. Over the years, we've helped a diverse array of leaders make meaningful change—sometimes via effective tweaks and other times through drastic overhauls. In either scenario, our overarching goal has always been the same: **transformation toward greater fulfillment and performance.**

This book is the latest step in our journey. In it, we extend to you over ten years of work and research. We give you an actionable perspective that helps you create a life that truly inspires and fulfills you, as well as helps you lead others in a transformative new way.

Our core approach to transformation—the approach that will be explained in the pages ahead—draws on cutting-edge neuroscience combined with research in cognitive, behavioral, positive, and sports psychology, sociology, leadership theory, philosophy and the realm of spirituality. It draws on work with a myriad of amazing people over the years—from Fortune 500 leaders, government employees, and non-profit managers to collegiate athletes, stay-at-home parents, and world-class educators. And it also draws on our broad spectrum of personal experiences. We are men of different generations from different countries who are in different phases of life. Our journeys and the ups and downs therein are the seeds from which this book has grown. We both have had many moments that have spurred us toward transformation. From facing personal struggles—one of us had to permanently leave his native country on the eve of revolution, while the other had to take care of his prescription drug-addicted father in the middle of the night—to dealing with career missteps—we've both lusted for status and experienced the emptiness that can come with it—we've been shaped by profound inflection points in our lives. And though, for both the clients we've worked with and ourselves, personal transformation hasn't always been easy, it has been possible. *It is possible.* And that's why we've created this book.

As we go through this journey together, you will see many stories of people who were able to find more meaning and fulfillment in their current circumstance through incremental but important changes. You will also see powerful stories of people who needed to make drastic changes in order to meaningfully realign their lives. Beyond that, you will learn more about the depths of our stories. Through these narratives and the framework we present, we will give you the tools to achieve greater happiness, performance, and fulfillment. Whether you foresee your transformation being big or small, sweeping or incremental, we've got you covered. And as you embark on your journey, not only will you begin to fundamentally change your own life, but you will also grow in your ability to meaningfully touch the lives of others. You will evolve as a leader. You will develop a presence and a skillset that will help you engage, empower, and sustainably motivate those around you.

The centralizing tenet of the book you are about to read is echoed in the work done by a former hospice care worker named Bronnie Ware. In her many years of tending to people at the end of their lives, people who recognized the preciousness of each remaining breath, she says that the most common regret they expressed was the following:

> I wish I'd had the courage to live a life true to myself, not the life others expected of me.[1]

The Inside-Out Effect is all about giving you the courage and skills to live that self-concordant life. It's about truly looking within and exploring what makes you tick. As you explore and begin living in line with that core part of you, your world will open up like it never has before. We are incredibly excited to take this journey with you.

MEET NATE

At 35, Nate has it all. Bachelor's and Master's degrees from UT-Austin. He works as a director for a large economic consultant firm in Washington, D.C. He drives a three-year old Audi A4 and is always well dressed. He lives with his wife and college sweetheart, Chloe, and their three children in a quaint neighborhood in Bethesda, Maryland. Though he frequently works long hours for his firm's Capitol Hill clients, he often makes it home by 8 pm to be greeted by welcome-home yaps from the family's Jack Russell Terrier, Izzie, and a usually tasty dinner concoction.

Nate makes a respectable salary (though he often labels it "modest" compared to some of his lobbyist friends' paychecks). With it, he is able to pay for math tutors for his children, as well as put money away for their college educations. He and Chloe invest religiously in their retirement funds, and after paying the household's current bills on time, they usually have expendable income left over. Over the last three years, he and Chloe were able to take the kids on a get-away vacation each year. Highlights included Disney World and the Outer Banks, North Carolina.

On the surface, Nate's life appears to epitomize success and happiness. He's got the job, the degrees, the significant other, the house, the loving family, the money, the car, and the dog. Given what most of us desire for our lives, it's easy to say that Nate has made it. His life appears to be a success. It truly seems, as we described at the beginning, like Nate has it all.

It may be surprising to learn, then, that Nate is not content. He does not feel like he's made it. In fact, *it* has always been hard for him to adequately define. For a while *it* was his Master's degree. Then *it* was his wedding day. Then *it* was climbing the ranks at his firm, then the house, then the kids, and so on. In fact, Nate has slowly realized that actually making *it* or reaching *success* is something he's never put a lot of thought into. Throughout most of his life, he has, almost by default, defined success—that *it* thing—by completing or achieving whatever short-term objective arose before him. Now that he has been at it for a little while, coupled with the fact that his list of obvious one- to three-year goals is slowly starting to dwindle, Nate can't help but feel lost—a little empty even. He has begun to look at the elements of his life—the same that, on paper, fit so nicely into society's definition of success—and wonder: "Is this really *it*?"

Nate has finally begun to explore his discontent. He has started to candidly look at how he's navigated his life to this point, and he has tried to be honest with himself about his current circumstances. As he has reflected, he has realized that the biggest thing that is gnawing away at him is the fact that he's still with a company that he joined eleven years ago under the auspices of it being a stepping-stone career move. When he joined, he was 24 and fresh out of his UT-Austin Master's program. He remembers being interested in gaining real-world experience about how public policy and economics truly intersect. He hoped that a positive experience would nurture his economics passion, prompt him to go back to school for a PhD within a few years, and eventually lead to a career as a published academic and university professor. As fate would have it, since Nate became enmeshed in the firm, he has never come up for air. The pay has been good and he, at least initially, enjoyed the challenges and pace demanded by his D.C. clientele. In fact, the longer he has stayed, the better the pay has gotten and the more influence he has had over which projects he is able to work on.

However, Nate is finally realizing that staying at the firm for over a decade has taken a serious toll. Over the last five years, he has slowly been worn down by the constant politics that pervade his work—many of the partners he works with have egos that fill up the entire room. What's more, when he finally comes home after long hours, he usually eats a late-plate alone in the kitchen while his children do homework in their rooms and Chloe reads in the family room.

Nate is tired; he is unfulfilled and worn out.

On one level, it has affected the energy he brings to the office, but even worse, it has affected his actual performance. Over the last few years, he's begun breezing through case write-ups, talking through client phone calls on autopilot, and has even begun to struggle to hit large project deadlines on time—something that never happened during his first several years at the company. He's also become increasingly ineffective as a leader. He's noticed more infighting on his team lately. The analysts he works with consistently seem tired and frustrated—almost as if they're feeding off of his discontented attitude. What was once a relatively upbeat and productive group of people more often seems like a group plagued by perpetual disenchantment. Though Nate tries to encourage them and resolve conflict when he can, the negativity seems more constant now than ever. Nate is finally beginning to be honest with himself; he is unhappy, unmotivated, and increasingly ineffective. He sees that his "what comes next?" approach to his job and success in general has mired him in the middle of petty D.C. politics with both colleagues and clients, has affected his job performance, has made him lose sight of his professional dream, and, most importantly, has made him miss far too much evening time with his children and Chloe. The rat race that once excited and enticed him is finally wearing him out.

Beyond leading to his mounting dissatisfaction with his job, Nate's perspective has also begun wearing on his relationships. Not only is it affecting his leadership at the firm, but it's also hurting his marriage. The reality is that he and Chloe have been struggling. They've begun to bicker more often than they ever have in the past. Whether it's about significant issues like him not making enough time for the kids (again, this ties back into his frustration with his career) or smaller irks like him forgetting to restock the milk when he drinks the last of a gallon before bed, they are frequently agitated with one another. And Nate is distraught about it. Their relationship, begun during their passionate, fun-loving college years, has been sustained by the hustle and bustle of starting their family and raising their kids. Things like buying their new family house, landscaping the yard, going to soccer practices, shuttling to dentist and doctor appointments, trying to fit in parent-teacher conferences, and lending the occasional hand with math homework have sucked them deep into the "what's next?" vortex and defined their relationship for years. However, just as Nate has become increasingly dissatisfied with his approach to his career, he's beginning to resent the status quo of their relationship. He can see that as he and Chloe have increasingly become fixated on what comes next—the next car, the bigger house, the new drapes, the next vacation—their relationship has suffered. What was once a source of such love and support—a constant pick-me-up after a long day—now frequently just adds to the heaviness of the day's events. They have lost sight of what's truly important to their relationship. They've lost sight of the importance of simply appreciating one another, of accepting and cherishing *what is* rather than *what's next*. He knows he absolutely loves Chloe, but he's struggling to figure out how to get them going again.

To top it all off, beyond his work and relationship issues, Nate has recently realized that his metabolism has started to slow down. Just last fall, he had to replace his whole pants wardrobe because his old ones no longer fit. He's managed to hold onto most of his dress shirts, but they too are starting to get a little tight around the buttons. Long gone are his Saturday morning runs with Izzie (poor Izzie is suffering with a little extra junk in her trunk too), and he hasn't returned to his old city league basketball team since he tore his ACL three years ago. Nate's beginning to realize that his salt-heavy, snack-on-the-go approach to food at the office coupled with long, static hours at his desk and general inactivity are finally starting to catch up with him.

As Nate has begun to introspect further, he knows something fundamental is missing. His discontent—his downright unhappiness with his job, performance, relationship, and fitness—leaves him wanting. He's a man who has everything yet lacks so much.

INTRODUCTION

Nate has an incredibly neat and idyllic life résumé but he's dissatisfied, unhappy, and increasingly ineffective. It doesn't add up, yet
it's a story we've all heard. More than that, it's a story that many of
us can relate to in one way or another.

According to a 2009 study, only 45% of Americans are satisfied
with their jobs.[1] While some would like to attribute these low figures to the 2008 economic crisis, the statisticians who have been
conducting this research for decades say that these percentages
are just the newest figures in an unsettling 20-year decline in
employee satisfaction and happiness.[2] And it's not just workplace
well-being that has suffered in recent years. Since the middle
of the 20th century, Americans' rates of depression have grown
more than tenfold.[3] Rates of alcoholism, suicide, and drug abuse
have all risen too.[4] All of this while our country has predominately
continued to grow and prosper. In the last 30 years, America's
inflation-adjusted GDP has more than doubled.[5] Our inflation-
adjusted median family income has grown significantly.[6] And
we're not alone. Countries around the world have begun to experience this crisis of meaning and fulfillment in the face of material and economic prosperity. It's long been noted in Europe. In
countries like Chile, South Korea, and China, though per capita
income has doubled in the last twenty years, surveys have shown
declines in life satisfaction amongst their people.[7] Around the
world, life expectancy is becoming longer than ever, yet many remain unfulfilled. Though most of us might not find ourselves in
Nate's exact situation, many of us have experienced unhappiness

> ½ of the world is in a crisis of poverty. The other ½ is in a crisis of meaning."
>
> –*Anonymous*

and ineffectiveness in the face of increasing monetary success, material wealth, and longevity.

Beyond facts and figures and on a very human level, nearly every one of us can relate to Nate's core feelings—the underlying lack of satisfaction and fulfillment—at some point in our lives. Of course, in certain cases these feelings are the result of incredibly difficult circumstances, and are therefore readily understandable and self-justifiable, at least for a while. Life can be disappointing and tragic. People get fired, households go bankrupt, and loved ones pass away. However, often these feelings become the ever-present themes in our lives. Arising subtly and slowly, they eventually become annoyingly persistent thorns in our sides. They appear out of frustration with our undesirable and seemingly unchangeable current circumstances. They creep into and spoil our life's triumphant moments. Or frequently, they are the result of uncertainty and indecision about our future.

Outside of their effect on our emotional well-being, these feelings often influence the way we behave. They manifest themselves in how we act and show up in our day-to-day lives. Disappointment and sadness in one area of life can affect our performance in another. A bored engineer certainly works more slowly than his engaged and excited colleague. An unfulfilled and disenchanted salesman most assuredly closes fewer deals than his motivated counterpart. As Nate has experienced, a void of meaning can affect our ability to lead others, connect with our families, and maintain our physiological health.

Whether you are currently in one of these difficult stages of life or you are simply yearning for a way to ratchet your performance and sense of fulfillment up another notch, this book is for you. This book is about transforming your life toward greater meaning and performance. In the pages that follow, we will help you unveil new possibilities all around you. We will help you find new avenues for growth and meaning at work as well as at home. And we'll help you do it in a way that's lasting and feasible. Although we're certainly not against drastic breakthrough changes, there is no "impulsively quit your job, sell your possessions, and move to the other side of the world" requirement to what we're talking about. We don't subscribe to the idea that a series of impulsive, sweeping changes are the key to repairing any of your current dissatisfaction or ineffectiveness. Despite what society often tells us, greater fulfillment is not about quickly jumping to what's new. It's not about the get-a-new-house/spouse/job/gadget mantra that pervades our culture. As Nate has realized, it's not about tirelessly answering the *what's next?* question. The reality is that it's quite the opposite. *The reality* is that greater personal fulfillment and performance start within. The change that brings about true fulfillment is rooted in self-awareness and personal alignment. And when this change happens, it happens from the inside-out.

THE INSIDE-OUT EFFECT

All too often we lead our lives from the outside-in. We pursue things, people, and jobs for their status and appearance, or because they're endorsed by our parents, friends, colleagues, or advisors. We make surface-level goals and we figure out how to go after them. If you really think about it, when it comes to life choices, we are quite proficient at answering questions like "what?" and "how?" The problem is that we're often not as competent with the "why?"[8] It's this struggle, this lapse in our perspective, which eventually leads to our dissatisfaction with our life's trajectory.

In order to curb the unfulfillment and underperformance that often accompanies prolonged living from the outside-in, we must turn our life paradigm on its head and begin living from the inside-out. We must start with the "why?" When we do this, we are able to pause the hurricane of our external world and purposefully look within. As we cultivate our self-awareness, we are able to make more authentic choices. The things we do and the directions we pursue become internally driven and, accordingly, more resonant and meaningful to our true selves. We become more resolute, more purposeful, more fulfilled, and more committed to our work and our relationships. We become aligned. The new fulfillment, energy, and commitment we encounter when we live from the inside-out is called the Inside-Out Effect.

Over the course of this book, we will give you a road map to achieve the Inside-Out Effect in your own life. In so doing we will present a toolkit for facing life's dissatisfactions and stagnations and transforming your life toward greater performance and fulfillment. Titled **KNOW-BE-LEAD**, our Inside-Out Effect framework addresses change from beginning to end, literally from the inside-out (see Figure 1). It contains techniques for increasing self-awareness, identifying core values, establishing meaningful goals, building new habits, and *leading* transformation in yourself and others.

We are all leaders. We are the leaders of our own lives and our own decisions. Leadership is not just about the number of people who report to you every day. It's about owning the autonomy you have over your own actions. Though we sometimes skirt the responsibility, when it comes to our life's trajectory, the buck stops with us at the end of the day. Then there's the traditional definition of leadership. We all have a hand in that too. Whether we're cognizant of it or not, we all have a sphere of influence. We influence and affect others all the time. As such, we have the ability to daily empower others toward greater effectiveness and fulfillment as well, to touch their lives in meaningful ways. Don't forget it. We believe deeply in the everyone-as-leader paradigm and have strongly woven it into the KNOW-BE-LEAD fabric.

As we explained in the Preface, KNOW-BE-LEAD is forged from innumerable hours of research; work with hundreds of clients, managers, athletes, consultants, educators, and executive coaches; as well as from the depths of our own experience. We've experienced its power in our own lives as well as the lives of the people we work with, and we are now excited to extend it to you.

THE INSIDE-OUT EFFECT

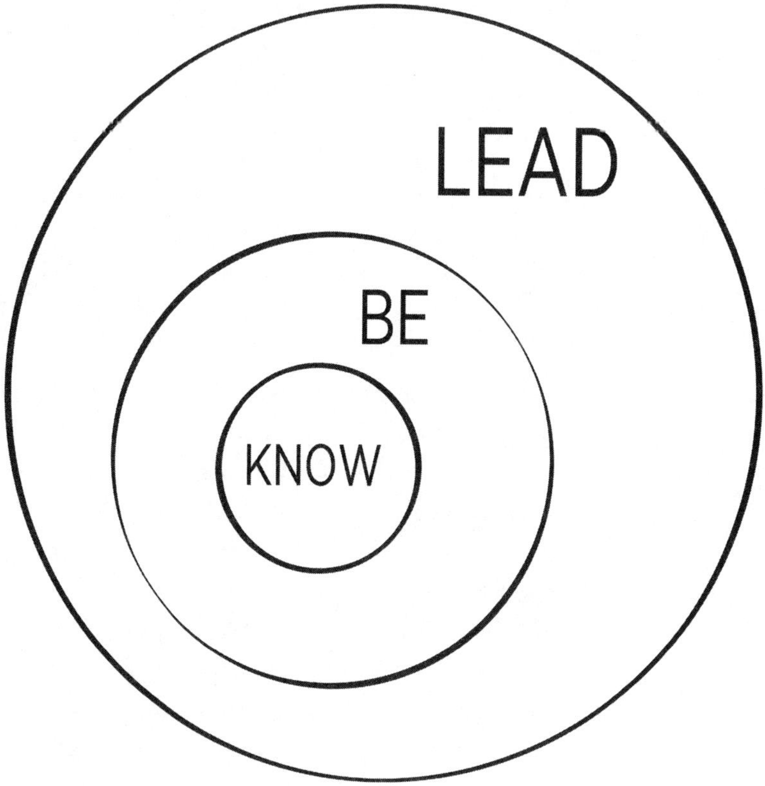

FIGURE 1

If you commit to this process, we promise that, little by little, you will find more purpose in your life, more happiness in the world around you, and greater performance for both yourself and those you lead and affect every day.

KNOW-BE-LEAD AND LIVING YOUR CALLING

KNOW-BE-LEAD is a three-part framework backboned by three essential questions:

1. Who do I, at my very core, know myself to be?
2. Who am I actually being day-to-day?
3. Am I authentically leading those around me?

As we go through it in the pages ahead, we'll give you the tools to honestly introspect, courageously pursue change, and more effectively lead yourself and others.

The underlying philosophy of KNOW-BE-LEAD has existed for years, which is a good thing because we've realized that there's more than a little bit of wisdom in the centuries of human consciousness that precede us. Across time, cultures, academic fields, and ideologies, this theme has been given labels such as being in your element, reaching a state of enlightenment, being in the zone, and finding a state of flow. Though these are powerful descriptors, each with its own set of nuances and all of which allude to an optimal state of being (whether for a moment or for a lifetime), we use the phrase *living your calling* as the underlying theme of the KNOW-BE-LEAD framework. We prefer *living your calling* because it evokes the idea of vocation, of deep-rooted personal purpose. We use it on a very personal level to describe fundamental passions that burn within. When you live your calling you inherently lead a more meaningful and fulfilled life because you are acting in accordance with what makes you tick. You are turning inward and, perhaps for the first time, really *listening*. Ultimately, living your calling means living your life—both professionally and personally—in alignment with who you truly are. It is the indicator of truly embodying the Inside-Out Effect.

"Who you truly are." We openly admit that this phrase can appear a little heavy—if not downright sentimental. But the truth is that honest self-knowing is essential to living a meaningful and fulfilling life. It is essential for inner-outer alignment and for genuinely interacting with and leading others. "Knowing who you truly are" is a weighty statement, but it's weighty because self-knowing is difficult to pursue and achieve. Many people, rather than engaging in the challenging, often emotionally exhausting process of self-discovery, would rather stay comfortable on the surface and scoff at anyone's attempt to dig beyond "the obvious." Think for a moment. We're sure you can easily think of at least a few people, perhaps siblings, aunts or uncles, friends, classmates, colleagues, or acquaintances, who would have such a reaction. Who knows, maybe you yourself tend to be one of those scoffers who finds it difficult to dedicate sincere energy to life's heavier questions. If you are, it's okay! We don't expect everyone to jump out of their seats at the idea of self-exploration. We do believe, though, that regardless of who you are, you are interested in becoming a happier, more fulfilled, and higher performing person. In that vein, we eagerly ask you to explore this difficult yet fulfilling topic with an open and curious mind. We're confident that what you find will be life-changing.

WHY IT MATTERS—THE EVIDENCE

When you've found and are living your calling, Things. Are. Easier. They're easier because, once you have aligned your actions with who you are, you've created a personal path of least resistance—you've consciously crafted an external reality that *fits* with your internal self, resulting in minimal internal friction. In his book

Happier, Harvard researcher Tal Ben-Shahar cites studies by psychologist Amy Wrzesniewski on professionals who experience their work as a calling and comes to the conclusion, "For a person experiencing work as a calling, work is an end in itself. While the paycheck is certainly important and advancement is too, he primarily works because he wants to. He is motivated by intrinsic reasons and experiences a sense of personal fulfillment; his goals are self-concordant."[9] People living their calling approach life with a sense of optimism and positivity—they are invigorated by the work that they do. The same is true for those living their calling in their personal lives. Relationships you have, hobbies you pursue, children you raise, and problems you encounter can all be navigated with an energy and a degree of effortlessness that wouldn't be there otherwise.

As you work through KNOW-BE-LEAD and get closer to experiencing the Inside-Out Effect, not only does your performance become easier, it also becomes better. Over the last fifteen years, the positive psychology and neuroscience fields have exploded with an enormous amount of ground-breaking research that has clearly showcased that approaching your career with a sense of meaning, happiness, and intrinsic positivity—that is, living your calling—improves your performance. In fact, studies have shown that people who approach their work with optimism and purpose are more creative, productive, produce higher quality results, and, in the long run, earn more.[10] Optimistic salespeople outsell pessimistic salespeople by 37%.[11] Employees who feel appreciated by their bosses, who feel like their work matters, increase their productivity by 31%.[12] People who find a sense of meaning and joy in their daily jobs are up to three times more creative than their colleagues.[13] According to Harvard-trained positive psychology expert Shawn Achor, "Over the past decade, scientists have made a revolutionary finding: happiness is actually the precursor to success, not merely the result of it . . . in fact, every single business outcome improves when a brain is set to positive as opposed to negative, neutral, or stressed."[14]

This makes sense on an intuitive level as well. If you spend your time doing things you're passionate about and things that you find energizing and uplifting, you are likely to spend a lot of time doing them—at least more time than the people who find those tasks less enthralling. And the more time you spend doing these things, the more proficient you will become at them. While this is fairly obvious, it is also well documented. Neuroscientists and psychologists have observed the time-spent-enhances-ability effect with athletes, educators, artists, writers, and skilled people from countless other professions.[15] It has also been showcased by Malcolm Gladwell in his book *Outliers*. He talks about the overwhelming importance of time spent practicing a task or skill in determining one's ability in that task or skill; specifically, he drives home the point that 10,000 hours of practice are necessary to achieve mastery in a particular area.[16] What a blessing: After a while, our passion-time cycle will result in greater proficiency, expertise and, thus, performance ability. If we truly commit to the things we love, we're bound to become skilled performers. Hence, by beginning to live your calling—that is, by beginning to build into your life the things that resonate most—not only do you experience more personal fulfillment, happiness, and positivity, you also experience better performance.

IT TAKES WORK

Don't get us wrong, just because you work hard to increase your self-awareness and begin pursuing things that matter most to the true you, it doesn't mean you won't face challenges or that you won't struggle. Reaching the Inside-Out Effect by living your calling might appear straightforward on paper, but it can be quite difficult in real life, especially in the early stages. That's because, for most of us, successfully living our calling requires change. And let's face it, change is hard.

"People resist change." It's one of the most common adages our society uses to explain why change efforts—be they political, organizational, or personal—often fail. It only takes a quick reflection back to last year's failed New Year's Resolution or last night's cookie splurge to find easy personal examples that support this statement. Beginning to live your calling can certainly be one of these difficult changes. It requires self-honesty that only comes through sincere commitment. It requires a willingness to try new endeavors and experiences—you often have to be open to putting yourself in unforeseen and sometimes uncomfortable situations to learn about the true you. Most of all, it requires courage. Courage to acknowledge the need for change. And then truckloads of more courage to implement that change.

Amid all of the difficulty surrounding change, there are several silver linings. The first is that, once you begin to step toward your calling, the change will progressively gain momentum. Remember, you're moving away from internal frustration and friction and into personal alignment—it's only natural to keep going. Eventually, with enough time and dedication, the change to living your calling not only becomes easy but it also makes so much sense. The second reassurance is that beginning to live your calling doesn't mean you have to overhaul your life. The vast majority of people we've worked with have been able to find significantly more meaning and fulfillment without having to leave their current company, relationship, or geographic location (as we said earlier, this is not a book about impulsively quitting your job and moving to a Himalayan monastery). The final reassurance is that we are here with you. The rest of this book is as much about ensuring your success as it is about articulating our framework for helping you live your calling. After all, you can read and understand KNOW-BE-LEAD, but if you can't implement it, we have failed. **More than anything, we want you to succeed. We want our framework to impact your life.**

Going forward, it's important to remember that KNOW-BE-LEAD is neither a magical quick fix nor a miracle pill. And it's no panacea—as humans, even after learning and applying this framework, we will all still experience ups and downs. However, with time and hard work, we can apply KNOW-BE-LEAD and steadily progress. Our "ups" will get higher and longer while our "downs" will get shallower and shorter. When we approach KNOW-BE-LEAD as a continuous process, as an actionable perspective, we work our way toward a more meaningful, high-performing and fulfilled life.

OUR ASK: A GROWTH MINDSET

We have one main ask of you as you embark on the KNOW-BE-LEAD process. Actually, it's an ask we'd like to make of you throughout this book and as you pursue your calling going forward. And that ask is that you strive to cultivate a growth mindset.

Somewhat self-descriptive, a "growth mindset" is a term coined by Stanford psychologist Carol Dweck.[17] A researcher on motivational and developmental psychology, Dweck's work on the power of mindset categorizes people into two basic camps: those with a growth mindset and those with a fixed mindset. People with a growth mindset believe that abilities can be developed and cultivated. They embrace challenges, persist in the face of obstacles, learn from criticism, and see effort as the path to mastery. Fixed mindset folks, on the other hand, view abilities as static and innate. They tend to avoid challenges, give up easily when faced with obstacles, ignore useful negative feedback, and see effort as fruitless.

"You always pass failure on the way to success."
–Mickey Rooney

Since they feel like their abilities—and in many ways, worth—are immutable, people with a fixed mindset shy away from things that are difficult. To try something difficult and fail is devastating for fixed mindset people because they see that failure as a permanent label on their unchangeable set of skills and behaviors. They see it as a permanent label of failure on who they are. People with a growth mindset take the opposite approach. For them, a difficult challenge presents an opportunity to learn and develop. They realize that learning, improvement, and change are iterative processes that take time and a willingness to persevere. And they don't take setbacks personally. Check out the following inner dialogue between a growth mindset (GM) and a fixed mindset (FM) when faced with a challenge:[18]

> **FM:** *"Are you sure you can do it? Maybe you don't have the talent."*
>
> **GM:** *"I'm not sure if I can do it now, but I think I can learn with time and effort."*
>
> **FM:** *"What if you fall short—you'll be a failure."*
>
> **GM:** *"Most successful people had failures along the way. If I stumble, I'll just try to pick myself back up."*
>
> **FM:** *"How about this? If you don't try, you can protect yourself and keep your dignity."*
>
> **GM:** *"If I don't try, I automatically fail. Where's the dignity in that?"*

As you can see, a growth mindset is a mindset of resilience and opportunity. It's a perspective where we let go of our vehement "positive" and "negative" judgments and open ourselves up to a journey of change and progress. Sure, with a growth mindset we might still hear things on some kind of positive-negative spectrum, but our focus can quickly go beyond that. It can quickly go to a space of *what can I learn from this?* and *how can I improve?*[19]

We request a growth mindset from you going forward. It will help you stay resilient over the sometimes-challenging process of beginning to live your calling. Though it won't always be easy, please try. Try to find and hold onto the learner within. Try to be open to the new challenges and opportunities that present themselves over the course of KNOW-BE-LEAD. Quiet your inner critic, judge, and pride. Acknowledge that **failure is part of learning**—as is picking yourself back up again. We've included a table of growth versus fixed mindset traits for your reference (Figure 2). Come back to it whenever you need to. Use it to catch the fixed mindset dialogue when it creeps up on you over the course of this process. Use it to reinforce your growth mindset and, like the example above, push back on your fixed mindset thoughts. Most of all, use it to remind yourself that change is possible.

GROWTH MINDSET	FIXED MINDSET
Positive	Cynical
Resilient dedication	Whimsical
Open to new things	Closed off
Courageous	Fearful/Self-doubtful
Present	Distracted
Honest	Hesitant

FIGURE 2

OUR AIM

We have large goals. We are obsessed with that smack-you-in-the-gut, look-yourself-in-the-mirror question: *Am I fulfilled by the life I'm living?* No beating around the bush. No sidestepping. We aim to bring you face to face with the questions that often lurk in the back of our minds, such as *Am I performing in my job and my life to the best of my ability? Do I consistently show up as the best version of myself? Does my professional success always have to come at the expense of my personal fulfillment? Does the way I conduct myself positively affect those around me? Am I influencing and leading others genuinely?* The great news is that we have high hopes for you, your fulfillment, and your ability to succeed. Beyond hopes, we have confidence. Whether it requires a significant change or subtle but important tweaks to your current way of life, we know that working through KNOW-BE-LEAD and living in greater alignment with your calling will have a positive impact on how fulfilled you feel. By striving for the Inside-Out Effect, all of us take the energy-zapping, mundane aspects of our lives and transform them into situations that empower us and give us purpose. We wade through all the noise and distractions—our impulsive emotions, our technological ADD, our mental ups and downs, the weekly gossip, and our ever-changing wants—to discover the power, freedom, and fulfillment that come when we live in alignment with our core values, with our true selves. And, as we've discussed, when you do this, your performance and ability to lead will improve drastically.

For the remainder of the book, we will progress through the KNOW-BE-LEAD framework and grow closer to achieving the Inside-Out Effect. In KNOW, we'll help you cultivate your self-awareness, identify your core values, and define success—or, as Nate would say, "making it"—on your own terms. In BE, we'll take you through the roadblocks that stand in the way of your sustained fulfillment and the mechanics of successful change implementation. We'll help you anticipate and overcome the friction you have around beginning to live more in line with your call-

> "If an egg is broken from the outside, life ends. If an egg is broken from within, life begins. Great things always begin from within."
> –Unknown

ing. Lastly, in LEAD, we'll help you discover how your authentic leadership has the power to transform the way you lead others—from your colleagues to your family. In the pages ahead, we'll share powerful stories of and quotations by famous and everyday people alike. We'll offer you windows into the realm of neuroscience called Brain Bites. We'll give you tools to drastically change how you experience your current job and life in general. We'll show you how, no matter your age or situation, *meaningful change is possible*. If you can try your best to commit to a growth mindset—that is, commit to positivity, dedication, openness, honesty, and a hearty dose of courage—we promise to give you a framework that will help you experience more fulfillment and performance across your life. Let's do this.

LEAD

BE

KNOW

STEP ONE

KNOW:
WHO AM I?

CHAPTER 1

Begin the Search, Avoid the Pitfalls

Before we can change our behaviors, our perspectives, and the way we affect and lead others, we first have to know the direction in which we want to change. If we want to begin living our calling, we first have to know what that calling is. For most of us, in order to know what it is, we have to search for it and search for it earnestly. And we have to search within. Therefore, our framework starts with *KNOWING*. It starts with one of life's fundamental questions: *Who am I?*

As we touched on at the beginning, asking ourselves this question and starting the process of searching for our true selves can be difficult. It can be difficult to pursue because of societal and self-judgment, and it's difficult to succeed at because it's an involved and, in some sense, continuous process. Despite this difficulty, it's an essential starting point and is a question we are committed to helping you navigate in the pages ahead.

It may seem intuitive that the first step of our framework is to know yourself. After all, how can you live in self-alignment if you don't clearly know and understand yourself? To our surprise, we've found that many approaches dedicated to increasing fulfillment—lots of them interesting and powerfully insightful—omit this step. Often people are encouraged to jump straight to goal definition, the change process, and new behaviors. Although there's nothing

> "As long as anyone believes that his ideal and purpose is outside him, that it is above the clouds, in the past or in the future, he will go outside himself and seek fulfillment where it cannot be found. He will look for solutions and answers at every point except where they can be found—in himself."
>
> –Eric Fromm

intrinsically negative with these starting points, we find them sub-optimal. As Chip and Dan Heath note in their book *Switch*, in a change scenario "what looks like resistance is often a lack of clarity."[1] Knowing yourself maximizes clarity, and therefore maximizes the chance that you'll have a successful, low-resistance change process. When you have a firm grasp on who you truly are, you will fully understand the nature of your calling. You will set your sights in the right direction and pursue life changes that have the highest probabilities of bringing you greater fulfillment. You'll feel more alive, more motivated and you'll perform better.

Now, back to the question itself: *Who am I?* It's a big one. It's a question that is frequently met with both intrigue and fear. It's intriguing because its answer holds the potential for revelation and understanding. The idea of deeper self-awareness and greater personal meaning are certainly alluring. On the other hand, for many of us, meddling with this question can seem a bit like opening Pandora's box. We're scared of what we might find (we'll talk more about fear later). We might discover beliefs, values, and dreams that are in opposition and create dissonance with the reality we live in. Or, in a scenario that is equally unnerving, we may initially find a void of meaning, an absence of any clear sense of our core values or truest passions. Digging away at who we are and what we value can make us simultaneously curious and terrified, and regardless of your prevailing emotion, it requires a lot of work.

So how do you begin to answer this question without being completely overwhelmed? The answer in a nutshell is bit by bit. However, to break this question down further, we'll talk later in KNOW about a series of techniques and practices for really grappling with it. We'll talk about quick diagnostics for getting general personality and temperament indicators as well as more in-depth routines for uncovering and solidifying your core beliefs and values. However, for now, we'd like to take a crucial first step that provides a lot of clarity during this initial phase of self-exploration: determine who you are not.

WHO YOU ARE NOT

Several years ago, we were on a break during a Stanford leadership training program and were chatting with one of the attendees, Chris Ferry. As we talked, Chris explained that she had spent many years as nurse in the Intensive Care Unit at Stanford Hospital but had made a career shift to work with mentally ill inmates in the Santa Clara county jail system. Taken aback, the first thing we could mutter was, "Wow, how can you handle working in prison?" After pausing for a second with a knowing look in her eye, she insightfully replied, "You know, in some form or another, we are all in prison."

Chris's words during that conversation struck a deep chord with us. In addition to their innate wisdom and depth, they embody the core theme of beginning to explore who you are not: identifying and breaking out of our identity prisons. Let's explore some of the most common identity pitfalls we use to confine and limit ourselves. Let's explore who you are not.

YOU ARE NOT YOUR STORY

At the moment we are born, we begin breathing. We immediately begin having experiences and, within a few years, start logging memories. Slowly, we begin to craft these experiences and their

21

> "Holding a grudge is letting someone live rent-free in your head."
>
> –Unknown

associated memories into a story—the story of who we are.

Our stories are usually the result of life moments that affected us in some noteworthy way. Over the course of our lives, we each have a range of experiences, from successes to mistakes, moments of pride to moments of embarrassment. In all of these moments we have *what happened* and we have *our spin*. In other words, something big occurred, objectively, and in response, we made a choice and told a *story* about *who I am*, subjectively.[2] We give weight and meaning to our pasts via our stories. We try to tie the *what happened* explicitly to *who we are*. In fact, our society is fond of the phrase, "these things in my past have made me who I am today." It's a phrase most of us accept and understand without hesitation. It's funny, though, how we tend to misplace so much of the essence of *who I am* in events of the past, events that we've responded to with subjective and often times subconscious identity choices. Just because a few mean children laughed at you in 2nd grade when you were reading a poem out loud to the class doesn't mean that you're inept or that you're a lousy public speaker. However, many of us trick ourselves into thinking that it does because that's the story we tell ourselves in our heads. We latch onto events of the past—particularly the ones that we perceive as profoundly negative. We identify, sometimes forever, with the stories we told ourselves during momentous past events. Beginning at the ripe age of three, Behnam started crafting a story that would limit him for the entire first half of his life.

About the Authors: Behnam's Identification with His Story

When I was very young, barely three-and-a-half actually, my mother and father divorced. As is common in Iran, my brother and I continued living with my dad after they split. Within a few months, my father remarried. Even though I was a young child, I remember watching it all happen from the sidelines. I remember my dad's new wife coming up to me after their wedding. She sat down next to me on the stairs of our house and said, "You can call me 'Mom.'" Though I'm now sure her comments were based out of love and kindness, at the time they only accentuated how turbulent and unfair life seemed to suddenly be. Over the course of a year, I went from having what I perceived as a stable and comfortable family to watching a divorce, remarriage, and new lady waltz into my life as my "Mom." I didn't know it then, but my dad and "Mom" would soon start having children of their own—after a few years, I would be one of five clamoring for my father's attention. I slowly began telling myself the story that life was uncertain, harsh, and unfriendly. Though I wouldn't recognize it until much later in life, I decided in that moment that I would have to be a fighter to make it—things were not going to be easy, the world was cruel, and, certainly, nothing would be handed to me. Specifically, as I grew up, I turned my attention to my studies. I dedicated myself to my schoolwork and focused intensely on getting top-tier grades. After all, my father was Harvard-educated; in order to rise above the clamor of my now gigantic group of brothers and sisters and gain his love and attention, I strived to achieve, achieve, achieve—achieve for his love; achieve for his affection; achieve to make it in this unfriendly world.

As fate would have it, this worldview and the subsequent decisions I made about who I was and what I valued were strengthened and perpetuated by the countrywide tumult of the Iranian Revolution. Seventeen at the time, I became an overnight revolutionary, fighting for democracy and the progression of my birth country. However, the revolution soon took an unexpected turn. Things got out of control quickly—my high school was closed down, martial law was instituted, and the Tehran airport was on the brink of shutdown. I realized that if I didn't leave instantly, I might never be able to pursue my education and life dreams. In the blink of an eye, I dropped everything and left the country on the last flight before the airport was shut down. Once again, I was able to reinforce my story that the world was an incredibly cruel and dangerous place. The events of the revolution reinforced my view of myself as a survivor and fighter. It showed me how everything you had could be wiped out in an instant. It taught me to protect, be conservative, and assume the worst.

In the years that followed, I held onto the lessons I had created around my past. I withdrew within myself, hid behind my academic pursuits, and strove to make my father proud. It wasn't until years later, when I became unexpectedly miserable in the midst of my greatest career and academic success (getting my PhD, teaching at a world-renowned school, working with high-profile clients in my private practice), that I recognized how much I defined myself based on the stories from my past. Since that time, I have practiced letting go of my story. I have decoupled the reality of who I am from the stories I used to tell about myself and the world around me. I have taken the three-and-a-half-year-old me and seventeen-year-old me out of my driver seat. As a result, I have been able to breathe fresh air into my life. My world is now a place that abounds with love and possibilities. Letting go of my story has enabled me to stop focusing on simply surviving via self-serving pursuits. It has given me the audacity to dream big—to live a life of service attempting to transform the lives of one hundred million people around the world before I die.

The fact of the matter is that our story is not linked to *who I am*. We try to fool ourselves, though, into thinking that it is. We convince ourselves that our story contains the essence of our true self when, really, all it is is a subjective narrative we play over and over again in our minds. See Figure 3 for an illustration of this confusion.

WHAT HAPPENED: OUR STORY:

PARENTS DIVORCE.
EXPERIENCE SADNESS.
FATHER REMARRIES.

TRUE LOVE DOESN'T EXIST.
PEOPLE ARE INHERENTLY
UNTRUSTWORTHY.
THE WORLD IS CRUEL
AND UNFAIR.

The mistake we make:

"I"

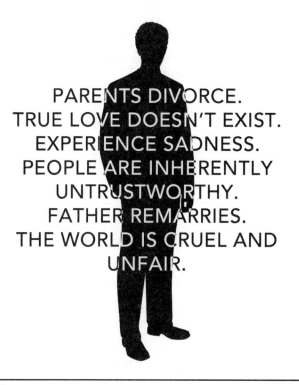

PARENTS DIVORCE.
TRUE LOVE DOESN'T EXIST.
EXPERIENCE SADNESS.
PEOPLE ARE INHERENTLY
UNTRUSTWORTHY.
FATHER REMARRIES.
THE WORLD IS CRUEL AND
UNFAIR.

FIGURE 3

Our story is the spin we put on our pasts. If we eliminate the story, we wipe the canvas of our subjective interpretations clean. We are liberated. When we realize that we are not our story, we quiet the critical narrator in our heads. We render our pasts powerless—nothing but an objective history of *what happened*. We free ourselves to answer *who am I?* in the only place we can—here and now.

A Man Who Let Go of His Difficult Story

Recognizing and accepting that the story we tell about past events doesn't have to define who we are can be difficult. It frequently means letting go of long-standing opinions, feelings, and, often, resentments. No matter how big of a hurdle that may seem to you, it can be done. For proof, we need look no further than one of the greatest leaders of our time, Nelson Mandela.

At the age of 46, Nelson Mandela was imprisoned by South Africa's apartheid government for leading violent resistance to their rule. He would spend the next twenty-seven years of his life in prison—the first eighteen of which were spent in a labor prison on Robben Island. During his first few years on the island, Mandela was under extreme physical and psychological pressures and at times felt an overwhelming resentment toward the people and institutions that took away his freedom. He was forced to toil in a lime quarry day after day under the supervision of guards who were often cruel and unabashedly hateful. As he settled into Robben Island, Mandela recounts that he and his comrades came "face to face with the realization that our life would be unredeemably grim."[3]

Despite this, Mandela gathered the will and courage to go on year after year. In time, he was able to let go of his angry and vengeful story; he was able to forgive those who took away his life and freedom. He eventually realized, "holding resentment is like drinking poison and hoping it will kill your enemy." As Mandela began to let go of the anger and outrage he associated with his past, he opened himself up to the new possibilities in his present.

> I am the master of my fate: I am the captain of my soul."
>
> –William Ernest Henley, one of Mandela's largest sources of inspiration on Robben Island

When he was finally released from prison, he said, "I greet you all in the name of peace, democracy, and freedom for all. I stand here before you not as a prophet but as a humble servant of you, the people. Your tireless and heroic sacrifices have made it possible for me to be here today. I therefore place the remaining years of my life in your hands."[4] He created a clean slate for himself and for his country by wiping clean the spin he put on his past. As you probably know, Mandela went on to become the first South African president elected in a fully representative election and was the 1993 recipient of the Nobel Peace Prize. Through his forgiveness—his willingness to let go of the story he told about his past—he was able to bring hope to a nation long shrouded in darkness. He became an example for us all.

Brain Bite: Malleable Memories
The Way Our Stories Influence Our Memories

Not only do our stories change the way we perceive our true selves, they also have a profound impact on our neurobiology. Specifically, they can influence the way our brains store and recall memories.

You see, when we recall a past event, the process our brains go through is constructive, not reproductive. By that we mean remembering is not like pressing play on a DVD we've seen before. Instead, it's a process in which the brain must construct or reform the memory from the various regions it has been stored in.[5] It must re-connect the dots, so to speak. As researchers have found, when the brain goes about this constructive process, it often makes mistakes. It's prone to crisscrossing parts of the desired memory with pieces of other experiences, and is also highly susceptible to your **stories**, beliefs, knowledge, and state of being at the time of remembering.[6]

Depending on the story you tell yourself, you can drastically alter the memories in your head. You can fundamentally change seemingly certain *what happened* memories just by telling yourself stories on repeat. The problem with this is you start to confuse the reality of *what happened* with the subjective *spin* of your story. Over time, more and more elements of your story can seep into the seemingly infallible truth of *what happened*, therefore further solidifying the decisions you've made about who you are on error-prone and interpretive information.

CLEAN YOUR FISH TANK

A vivid analogy we like to use is called the Fish Tank Metaphor (see Figure 4). In it we describe each of our lives as the life of a single fish in a fish tank. When we are born, we're placed into a beautiful tank full of crystal clear water. However, as we grow and start having experiences, forming memories, and linking our identity to the things of the past through our stories, it's as if we start taking poops in our fish tank. *My mother seldom showed affection—I must be unworthy of love . . . poop! My grandparents got divorced—see marriage can't last forever . . . poop! I couldn't get a job after college in the industry I wanted—I knew I was a no-good engineer . . . poop!* After a while, maybe by our teenage years, maybe by the time we start our careers or, for some, maybe closer to retirement, our defecation builds up so much that we can no longer see the world around us. We have given our stories, our resentment of the past, and our fear of the future control over our identities and are swimming in a mess of our own creation. In order to transform our lives, we must clear out the poop. We must clean out our fish tank. When we realize that we are not the mess we've created, we can transcend it.

> " Most of the shadows of this life are caused by standing in our own sunshine."
>
> *–Ralph Waldo Emerson*

FIGURE 4

YOU ARE NOT YOUR APPEARANCE

Figuring out who you are not is all about differentiating yourself from common identity pitfalls. It's about letting go of your story, about recognizing and cleaning the poop in your fish tank. The trend continues with our next point: You are not your appearance. Your hair color, waistline, nose shape, car, salary, and purse brand have nothing to do with the true you. You are not the things you own, the looks you've inherited, or the status you seek. This point may seem obvious, but it is one of our most common identity pitfalls.

Our world is overflowing with examples of how we misappropriate people's identities based solely on their appearances. Tabloids, blogs, TV shows, social networks, and advertisements consistently bombard us with reminders of the importance of appearance. *You've truly made it when you can afford a luxury European car. That actress wears this perfume—if you want to be beautiful and charming like her, you should buy some.*

This isn't to say that we're completely unaware of the appearance-centric nature of our culture. Many people, it seems especially parents and teachers, try to push back on society's appearance obsession. When we're children, these people who care about us tell us things like, "It's what's on the inside that truly matters" or "You're beautiful inside and out!" They try their best to plant the seeds of finding your true beauty, your identity, within. Though they try, their words are often short-lived. Too many of us grow up and forget their message. We begin evaluating our homes through the lens of *Architectural Digest* and our success from the standpoint of *Fortune* magazine. We count our degrees, diamonds, and dollars. We try to appear smart and influential in front of our colleagues and friends. When we mistake *who we are* for *what we have* or *what we look like*, we create pain, division, and feelings of inadequacy between us and other people as well as within ourselves. One of the most famous speeches in the history of the United States crescendos on a line that speaks to this very point: "I have a dream that my four little children will one day live in a nation where they will not be judged by the *color of their skin* but by the *content of their character*."[7] Our society is still working toward the "one day" Martin Luther King Jr. spoke of nearly fifty years ago. As we all strive to discover the true content of our characters, we must disregard the color of our skin, our appearance, and our things in general, for they are not us.

> People are made to be *loved* and things are made to be *used*. The confusion in this world is that things are loved and people are used."
>
> –Unknown

YOU ARE NOT YOUR THOUGHTS

Though it can be difficult to grasp initially, you are not your thoughts. We understand the tension that often surfaces when digesting this concept for the first time. It's easy to think: *Thoughts seem so fundamentally linked to self-awareness and personal discovery. Aren't thoughts the internal voices that recognize and express your true self?* Though it might be counterintuitive, the answer is "no" the vast majority of the time. Allow us to explain. The majority of the time, we each have countless thoughts whizzing around within us, seemingly at random. They are focused, tangential, long, short, organized, disheveled, crisscrossing, and, more than anything, constant. Due to humans' negativity bias—that is, the propensity for negative events or thoughts to have a stronger pull on our attention[8]—these thoughts routinely try to suck us into thinking

31

> What a liberation to realize that the voice in my head is not who I am."
>
> –Eckhart Tolle

that they are us and that we *need* this, *want* that, or that we should *fear* this, or *aren't good enough* to accomplish that. And the fact of the matter is, try as we might, we cannot control them. Even the most self-controlled among us is no match for his or her thoughts. If you doubt this, try to resist the following image from appearing in your mind: a pink elephant. Although you may be tempted to deny it, the truth is that nearly every one of you just experienced at least a microsecond flash of a mental image of a bubblegum-colored Dumbo.

Being unable to control our thoughts is not fundamentally a bad thing. Instead, it's one of the strongest indicators that we are not our thoughts. The majority of our thoughts are like drummers that march along to the beat of their own drum, generally unyielding to our intermittent attempts at control. When we realize this separation—the gap between our thoughts marching around and ourselves—we realize that they are not us. We make a distinction: there are our thoughts and there is that part of us that can observe our thoughts. This realization is often called awareness or awakening. We are that awareness. We are not the noisy traffic-jam created by our thoughts.

Brain Bite: Automatic Thoughts
Constant, Innumerable Thoughts

The overwhelming majority of the thoughts and ideas that arise within our brains are generated via automatic (i.e., nonconscious) processes. That means that the electro-chemical highway that is your brain makes decisions or conjures thoughts before you can even consciously comprehend them. In fact, according to a 2008 study done by neuroscientists at the Max Planck Institute for Human Cognitive and Brain Sciences, your brain makes decisions 7 seconds before you're consciously aware of your choice.[9] Your brain is a powerful machine that's able to, in a given moment, simultaneously absorb approximately 11 million units of information, while you're only consciously aware of a maximum of 40.[10] Translation: the vast majority of what goes on in your head is done automatically, without your permission, and before it enters your consciousness. Accordingly, don't get too hung up on or over-identify with your cascade of thoughts.

Note: Even though this is the case, there is good news. As you'll see in BE, you can actually rewire a significant number of your brain's automatic processes to work in alignment with your calling! We'll show you how when we discuss behavior change and neuroplasticity.

YOU ARE NOT YOUR EMOTIONS

For reasons similar to you not being your thoughts, you too *are not your emotions*. As an objective point, this could prove difficult to accept. After all, you have probably tried to associate the emotions you often feel with certain truths about yourself. Perceiving yourself as someone who has a short temper, is aloof, or is always happy might be true about your current pattern of behavior, but is not part of your core self. Sure, through either nature or nurture, you have a certain attitude or perspective orientation—we are all a little bit different—yet you are not the emotions you experience at any given time. Since you have already seen that you are not your thoughts, the logic for you not being your emotions is really quite straightforward. In their truest terms, emotions are physiological reactions to thoughts. The short, heavy breaths and "boiling blood" of anger, the tears and sobs of sadness, the smiles and euphoria of joy, and the quick pulse of nervousness are all quintessential examples of emotions being your body's response to your thoughts at a given time. As extensions of automatic, non-you thoughts, emotions are fundamentally separated from who we really are. The woman who yells at her colleague for perceived favoritism at work is not you. The man who longs for a motorcycle like his friend's is not you. You can transcend those emotional identity pitfalls because who you truly are has already done so. In fact, it has always done so.

BRINGING IT TOGETHER: YOU ARE NOT YOUR EGO

All of these *who we are not* concepts are, in some way, functions of the human ego. Author Eckhart Tolle defines the ego as "the blueprint for dysfunction that every human being carries within."[11] He writes that the ego is, at its core, "an illusory sense of identity."[12] Simply put, Tolle shows how our egos attach themselves to external, peripheral, or impermanent things, and how most of us mistake the *I* in our *who am I?* search and lives in general for the egoic "I." We've spent this chapter debunking this egoic "I," exposing it and the pitfalls it presents. Though our egos identify with our stories, pasts, appearances, thoughts, and emotions, we are not these things.

Your true self is the aware you, the consciousness behind the noise. Like the Wizard of Oz hiding behind the curtain in the Emerald City, the true you—the *I* in *who am I?*—lives behind the curtain of your ego. It is the part of you that has the ability to zoom out from the cacophony created by your story, your appearance, and your constant whirlwind of thought and emotion to look upon yourself with honest perspective. By knowing who we are not, we can free ourselves from the egoic flood that tries to drown us on a daily basis; we can drill down to our true consciousness behind the noise (see Figure 5).

FIGURE 5

As we go through KNOW, it's as if we are able to wipe the slate of our perceived identity clean. We are freed from the spin we put on our stories, the behavior adopted because of our past or future, and the goals made because of our egoic thoughts and emotions. We are able to answer *who am I?* by turning to our own awareness, our own consciousness. Once we have the tools to explore it, we can find our calling.

Einstein's Wisdom—His Take on Who You Are Not

Albert Einstein once said, "The intuitive mind is a sacred gift and the rational mind is a faithful servant. We have created a society that honors the servant and has forgotten the gift." Though he might not have known it then, Einstein's words contained a fundamental truth that would carry forward into the 21st century—we still, today, live in a society that honors the rational mind. We live in a world that honors intense structure, bureaucracy, a glut of information, and analytics. And as we have just finished discussing, many of us honor and overly identify with our rational thoughts, stories, and narrow comparisons to others—all functions of the rational mind.

Einstein's words map nicely to one of the basic frameworks people often use to describe the main regions of the human brain—the right vs. left brain. Though contemporary neuroscience has showcased that the hemispheres of our brains are much more interconnected and codependent than we once thought, there are still general characteristics that can be ascribed to these regions and to our rational-intuitive split.

The rational brain, the brain with which most of the world operates and which we often overly identify with, focuses on the concrete, mechanical, categorical, and analytical. It interprets and creates an ordered world where it focuses on what is known, and makes rational evaluations and decisions based on past experiences. The intuitive brain, meanwhile, deals with the abstract and big-picture implications of life. It views the world as a changing and interconnected system in which possibility reigns supreme. The divergent characteristics of the two brains results in them having different primary emotions. The rational brain often gets bogged down in negativity and fear. It is careful and anxious, always on the lookout. The

36

intuitive brain, on the other hand, tends toward hope, curiosity, creativity, and peace. It makes connections between seemingly unrelated things and is able to see opportunity in nearly every situation (see Figure 6).

RATIONAL BRAIN	INTUITIVE BRAIN
Detail-oriented	Big-picture oriented
Expectations	Possibilities
Analytical	Creative
Conditioned by past	Focuses on present and future
Acknowledges	Appreciates
Overly cautious	Adventurous
Comprehends things (knows)	Sees the meaning in things (believes)
Negative emotion default	Positive emotion default

FIGURE 6[13]

The bottom line is that we have given our rational brains too much control. Most of us spend far too much time in our structured, analytical worlds, frequently missing opportunities to connect, grow, and create. Iain McGilchrist, a renowned psychiatrist and former neuroimaging researcher at Johns Hopkins University, says, "Today we live in a world which is paradoxical. We pursue happiness and it leads to resentment and it leads to unhappiness and it leads, in fact, to an explosion of mental illness . . . more information, we have it in spades, but we get less and less able to use it to understand, to be wise."[14] He even explains that despite our pursuit of freedom, we live in a world more monitored and policed than ever before. These unfortunate things are a result, in part, of our collective leaning toward and over-identification with our rational brains.

This isn't to say that the rational brain doesn't serve a purpose. It's essential for precise tasks such as solving problems and organizing strategies. It's incredibly useful for the development and use of language. It enables us to build magnificent tools and technologies. However, as Einstein said, it is the faithful servant. Our intuitive brain is the sacred gift. Many of us have forgotten that fact; we have misappropriated who we are. The core of who we are does not reside in our rational minds—it resides in our intuition.

THE TOOLS
A SUMMARY

- The first step toward greater self-awareness is clarifying who you are not.
- Strive to separate yourself from common pitfalls by realizing you are not your **story**, **appearance**, **thoughts**, or **emotions**.
- Liberate yourself by:
  - Cleaning the poop out of your fish tank.
  - Separating the *what happened* from *your spin*.
  - Trying to quell the urge to identify with and base your worth on things and comparisons to others.
  - Naming and differentiating yourself from your stream of thought and emotion. You are not the "voice in your head."
- Recognize that all of your identity pitfalls are the result of our collective "blueprint for dysfunction" called the ego. The true you is the awareness behind it.

CHAPTER 2

Exploring You

Now that we have successfully ruled out *who you are not*, it's time for us to explore the inner workings of *who you are*. It's time to get in touch with our intuitive brains, to earnestly explore the awareness that exists behind the shroud of our stories, appearances, thoughts, and emotions.

Before we begin our exploration, it's worth noting that learning about oneself is often a bit different than traditional learning. When you're learning to drive a motorboat or to become proficient in Excel, you're generally learning something you know you don't know (KDK), whereas when you commit to improving your self-awareness, you're often learning things you didn't know you didn't know (DKDK). The reason we bring this up is twofold. One, it's to ensure any of you who are thinking that you already know yourself pretty darn well that there's plenty to learn. And two, it's to inspire patience and repetition. Unlike learning to tie your shoes, learning about yourself is an iterative, evolving process that will consistently reveal new insights and discoveries. So, even though we're going to go through this chapter together now, it's a topic that you should revisit regularly going forward. You never know what you'll discover about yourself. For a graphical illustration of this point, see Figure 7 (KK = things you know you know).

> "Sometimes, you have to step outside of the person you've been and remember the person you were meant to be. The person you want to be. The person you are."
>
> –H. G. Wells

In the pages ahead, we'll discuss a variety of techniques and approaches for successfully looking within. Among the methods we present, our hope is that you will find a handful that work effectively for you. If a certain technique doesn't resonate or isn't particularly useful for you, don't worry. We all learn differently—especially when we are learning about ourselves. In fact, as you revisit this exploration over time you may find that the methods that are most effective for you change, and that's great. As with earlier in the book, we ask that you approach these techniques with a growth mindset—bring an open mind, energy, and honesty. And be ready to work. This isn't a PowerPoint at the office or a batch of brownies for your

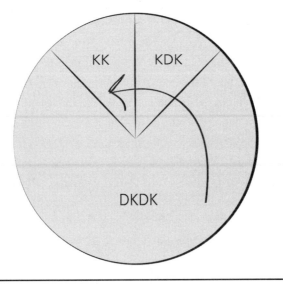

FIGURE 7

son's school bake sale. This is the exploration of *what makes you tick*. The adage "you get out what you put in" is never truer than it is with self-exploration; it's never been truer than it is at this moment. Let's do this right. The pages that follow are all about you flushing out the details of *who am I?* As your ability to confidently answer that question grows, so too does your ability to determine your calling. And, as we've said before, solidifying your calling is the first step toward greater fulfillment, performance, and transformational leadership. It's the first step toward reaching the Inside-Out Effect.

BEGINNING TO SEE: STRENGTHS—EVOKES—ELATES

Our centralizing tool for this chapter is called SEE. Standing for Strengths–Evokes–Elates, **SEE** is a three-part model that will help drive you toward defining your calling. As you can see in Figure 8, SEE is a three-circled Venn diagram that intersects on one's Calling Sweet Spot.

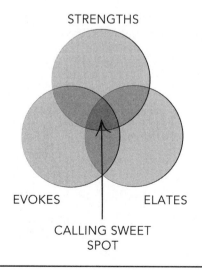

FIGURE 8

> "Knowing others is intelligence; knowing yourself is true wisdom. Mastering others is strength; mastering yourself is true power."
>
> –Lao Tze

As its name implies, the SEE process is all about finding the overlaps between your *strengths*, the things that *evoke* personal meaning, and the things that make you feel *elated*. The philosophy is really quite simple: When you combine the things that give you immediate joy with the things that give you sustained purpose and then combine those things with what you *are* or are *willing to work to be* good at, you have a recipe for your calling. Thus, the SEE model that backbones our self-exploration begins with extensive and repeated introspection—the thing we'll be striving for throughout this section—and ends with realization about the fundamental nature of our calling.

We encourage you to look at SEE as a template to be filled out as you go through the rest of this section (you can find a printable version on our website, www.theinsideouteffect.com). As you learn self-discovery techniques, write down your learnings in the context of SEE. List new strengths, chronicle things that evoke a deep sense of meaning, and scribble down experiences that elate you. It's worth noting that, before going on to any other KNOW technique, you can use SEE at face value for a good starting point. Feel free to brainstorm by SEE category in a simple and straightforward way before you get going on the rest of this section. It may seem pretty simple, but between thoughtful brainstorming and dedicated work in the rest of this section, the things you discover can be quite profound.

As you progress through the rest of this chapter and begin to find commonalities in your SEE results, we encourage you to thoughtfully examine each overlap. What does that strength-evoke commonality say about you? Which skillset does that intersection remind you of? What does the middle, Sweet Spot overlap indicate about the nature of your calling? As you do this, you may discover parts of yourself that you long ago put on the shelf. You may be reminded of invigorating experiences you once had that left an impact on your memory. Using SEE as the lens through which you approach all of these other techniques, you will learn about yourself in a powerful way. If you do this process genuinely, you will grow your self-awareness and, in the end, be able to clearly articulate the parameters of your calling and personal fulfillment.

On the next page, you'll find a SEE template. Before you go any further, please spend a moment with the diagram. Copy it onto a Post-it note or piece of paper. Leave it next to your computer, pin it to your bulletin board, or tape it to your wall. We want you to have this template as a repository for the things you learn about yourself over the course of this journey. Use it. Muck it up. Explore. What you find through using SEE and the forthcoming techniques can be life changing.

As we mentioned on the very first page, you can access most of our tools and exercises online at www.theinsideouteffect.com if you prefer not to write in your copy of the book. A large SEE diagram is available on the site if you'd rather download and print it.

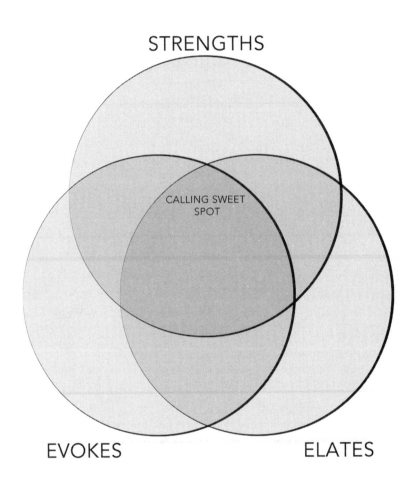

STRENGTHS

CALLING SWEET
SPOT

EVOKES

ELATES

THE ENNEAGRAM

We'd like to start by presenting a few tools aimed at providing an initial, top-down look at who you are. Specifically, we're going to zoom in on the overall orientation of your personality and perspective. We're the first to acknowledge that these first few methods are certainly not all-encompassing when it comes to answering *who am I?*, but they do provide a great first glance and, often times, a thought-provoking starting point.

The first technique we'd like to discuss is a personality diagnostic called the Enneagram. Developed in the mid-20th century, the Enneagram has roots in an array of ancient cultures. Literally meaning "nine-pointed figure" (*Ennea* means "nine" in Greek and *grammos* means "figure"), the Enneagram is a geometric figure that maps out nine fundamental personality types at its vertices. Of the nine types, no type is better or worse than another. By taking a brief survey (one of which we include at the end of this section), you can determine your type and see how it relates to the other eight types. This is helped in part by the Enneagram shape itself (Figure 9).

As you can see, each type (or number) has two edges coming out of it. These edges indicate the *functional* and *dysfunctional* directions for each type. In other words, one edge leads to the type that a given person becomes more like during difficult or uncertain times (at their worst), and the other leads toward the type that the same person becomes more like in times of personal safety and growth (at their best). For example, a Reformer often shows Individualist traits when under stress and Enthusiast traits when highly comfortable. This characteristic is one of the Enneagram's biggest advantages among personality diagnostic methods. It makes explicit the interconnectedness of the types, showcasing the overlaps and subtleties between multiple personality perspectives. It shows

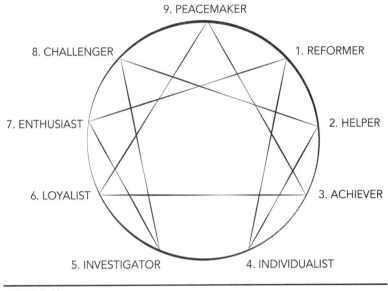

FIGURE 9[1]

how we all have a given range of orientations, each of which comes to the forefront in certain situations.

For example, someone who is an 8, often labeled the "Leader" or "Challenger," is generally self-confident and assertive. They are decisive, willful, and competent, which makes them powerful leaders and effective decision makers. Their potential downfall stems from their need to control their environment. When they feel threatened, they can become confrontational and domineering, sometimes taking advantage of weaker or more timid peers. When 8s are in stress, they move in their direction of dysfunction and can become secretive and afraid 5s, but when they're in a time of comfort and growth, they move in their functional direction and can become more open, caring 2s. As you can see in the following overview table (Figure 10), each type has a series of distinct characteristics. They have strengths and weaknesses, with no one type being better than another.

TYPE #	TYPE NAME	AT THEIR BEST	UNHEALTHY	SAVING GRACE	FUNCTIONAL DIRECTION	DYSFUNCTIONAL DIRECTION
1	Reformer	Wise, discerning	Self-righteous, severe	Capacity for reason	7	4
2	Helper	Deeply charitable, humble	Angry for being under-appreciated	Empathy	4	8
3	Achiever	Inner-directed, genuine	Hostile, indifferent	Wanting acceptance	6	9
4	Individualist	Hyper-creative	Dependent on others, self-victimize	Self-knowledge	1	2
5	Investigator	Visionary, pioneering	Hoard space, time, selves	Comprehend many views	8	7
6	Loyalist	Faithful, committed	Anxious, overreactive	Desire for connection	9	3
7	Enthusiast	In love with life	Escapist, impulsive	Optimistic, energetic	5	1
8	Challenger	Magnanimous	Aggressive, intimidating, controlling	Benevolence	2	5
9	Peacemaker	Receptive, reassuring	Helpless, checked out	See all sides of an issue	3	6

FIGURE 10[2]

47

About the Authors: Behnam's Enneagram Experience

My passion for the Enneagram comes not only through formal study and research, but also through numerous firsthand experiences. Over the course of the last ten years, I have used it with hundreds of friends, acquaintances, colleagues, students, clients, and my family and witnessed overwhelmingly positive results. I'll share two brief yet notable examples.

Not too long ago, the Polish prime minister sent fifty of Poland's top innovators to Stanford to study leadership. While they were here, I had the fortune of leading a session with them. During the session, we got into a discussion about leadership styles and approaches. As the conversation progressed, I realized that many of these Polish leaders—these professors, scientists, and entrepreneurs—were expressing similar viewpoints and cookie-cutter answers regarding leadership style. I felt like the discussion lacked depth and true value. Thus, I decided to interject and spent the next thirty minutes of our session on the Enneagram. The truth, I told them, was that they were much less homogenous than they thought. Though on the surface they might view themselves as people with the same perspectives, the reality was far more complex. I had them take a quick Enneagram diagnostic test and then divided them around the room by type. I then went around the room and described to each the core tendencies as well as the strengths and weaknesses of their types. Though it started slowly at first, I began to get more and more nods as I went around. They were amazed at the insights the Enneagram provided about who they were as leaders and as people. At the end of our discussion, many of them were excited to take the Enneagram back to their companies, organizations, and teams. Beyond that, many wanted to take it back and use it with their families.

Much like the Polish innovators, one of the first application areas I saw for the Enneagram when I first encountered it was with my family. At the time, my daughter was just entering her teenage years and, as many parents can relate to, things were a little turbulent between us. As I grew accustomed to the Enneagram, I pegged her for a 4 due to her creative nature as well as the range of emotions she was consistently feeling and expressing at the time. It turns out, after taking several diagnostic tests, she was a solid 8. Wow! What a revelation for me. My daughter, whom I had thought to be an individualist artisan was really a challenger. She was a leader whose desire for autonomy came from wanting to galvanize people rather than express herself creatively as I had anticipated. Learning her type helped both of us. It began to facilitate new and productive discussions and contributed to improving our relationship. My daughter has even begun to use it with many of her friends—she views it as a great aid in any relationship.

If you end up using the Enneagram to kick off your self-exploration process, keep in mind that it is not an ultimatum upon your personality and core self. It is a great indicator of many of your core tendencies and can be a powerful starting point for self-discovery, but don't let it confine you. Like with many personality diagnostic tools, people often mistakenly use the Enneagram as a way to permanently label themselves and others. They sometimes fall into the trap of using the Enneagram as a personal crutch or as an excuse to judge other people. Don't let that happen to you. The reality is that we are all incredibly dynamic beings who grow and change over time. Though your Enneagram personality type will give you a solid starting point, it certainly will not be all-encompassing when it comes to answering *who am I?* Fully answering that question is a long, iterative process that extends beyond any one method.

That said, we really encourage you to use and explore the Enneagram. It will give you a powerful and thought-provoking starting point for self-discovery. If you take your time and strive to be self-aware in your exploration of the Enneagram, we think you'll be surprised by some of the insights it provides.

To aid in your Enneagram journey, we've provided here the "Quick Enneagram Sorting Test" ("QUEST") by Enneagram experts Don Riso and Russ Hudson. It's a quick test to determine your Enneagram type with about 70% accuracy. As you take it, we ask that you make sure to be incredibly honest, open, and intuitive when answering. Don't let your egoic self take control as you answer. Don't choose answers based on who you desire to be or think you *should* be. We want this exercise to help you begin to dig at the true you, so please, strive to be in a state of awareness when you're answering. When you've completed the QUEST, please visit www.enneagraminstitute.com to explore your type (click "Type Descriptions" on the left menu bar). Several more in-depth diagnostic tests are also available on that site.

The Riso-Hudson QUEST[3]

This is a two-part test. Each part consists of three paragraph descriptions. For each part, read all three paragraphs carefully. When you're done with all three, rank the paragraphs from 3 to 1 in the order of which ones best describe your actual behavior (3 being the one that most describes you, and 1 being the one that least describes you). As with all of our KNOW techniques, self-honesty is an extremely important part of this process. Put yourself in a place of awareness and go with your gut reactions as you read. When you're done, go through the QUEST Interpretation exercise to determine your most probable Enneagram type.

PART I

RANK: **A.** I have tended to be fairly independent and assertive. I've felt that life works best when you meet it head-on. I set my own goals, get involved, and want to make things happen. I don't like sitting around—I want to achieve something big and have an impact. I don't necessarily seek confrontations, but I don't let people push me around either. Most of the time I know what I want, and I go for it. I tend to work hard and to play hard.

_____

RANK: **B.** I have tended to be quiet and am used to being on my own. I usually don't draw much attention to myself socially, and it's generally unusual for me to assert myself all that forcefully. I don't feel comfortable taking the lead or being as competitive as others. Many would probably say that I'm something of a dreamer—a lot of my excitement goes on in my imagination. I can be quite content without feeling I have to be active all the time.

_____

RANK: **C.** I have tended to be extremely responsible and dedicated. I feel terrible if I don't keep my commitments and do what's expected of me. I want people to know that I'm there for them and that I'll do what I believe is best for them. I've often made great personal sacrifices for the sake of others, whether they know it or not. I often don't take adequate care of myself—I do the work that needs to be done and relax (and do what I want) if there's time left.

_____

51

PART II

RANK: 1. I am a person who usually maintains a positive outlook and feels that things will work out for the best. I can usually find something to be enthusiastic about and different ways to occupy myself. I like being around people and helping others to be happy—I enjoy sharing my own well-being with them. (I don't always feel great, but I generally try not to show it!). However, keeping a positive frame of mind has sometimes meant that I've put off dealing with my own problems for too long.

RANK: 2. I am a person who has strong feelings about things—most people can tell when I'm upset about something. I can be guarded with people, but I'm more sensitive than I let on. I want to know where I stand with others and who and what I can count on—it's pretty clear to most people where they stand with me. When I'm upset about something, I want others to respond and to get as worked up as I am. I know the rules, but I don't want people telling me what to do. I want to decide for myself.

RANK: 3. I am a person who is self-controlled and logical—I don't like revealing my feelings or getting bogged down in them. I am efficient—even perfectionistic—about my work and prefer working on my own. If there are problems or personal conflicts, I try not to let my feelings influence my actions. Some say I'm too cool and detached, but I don't want my private reactions to distract me from what's really important. I'm glad that I usually don't show my reactions when others "get to me."

QUEST Interpretation

Now that you've completed your rankings above, please add your ranks for each 2-digit combination below. The results will indicate your three most probable Enneagram types (whichever type sums to "6" is your most probable type and the two that sum to "5" are your next most probable types). Once you narrow in on your most probable types, we encourage you to explore them further at www.enneagraminstitute.com.

2-DIGIT COMBO	ADD RANKS	TYPE	NAME & KEY CHARACTERISTICS
A1	_____	7	**Enthusiast:** Spontaneous, versatile, acquisitive, scattered
A2	_____	8	**Challenger:** Self-confident, decisive, willful, confrontational
A3	_____	3	**Achiever:** Adaptable, excelling, driven, image-conscious
B1	_____	9	**Peacemaker:** Receptive, reassuring, agreeable, complacent
B2	_____	4	**Individualist:** Expressive, dramatic, self-absorbed, temperamental
B3	_____	5	**Investigator:** Perceptive, innovative, secretive, isolated
C1	_____	2	**Helper:** Generous, demonstrative, people-pleasing, possessive
C2	_____	6	**Loyalist:** Engaging, responsible, anxious, suspicious
C3	_____	1	**Reformer:** Principled, purposeful, self-controlled, perfectionistic

MYERS-BRIGGS

The second technique we want to touch on is the Myers-Briggs Type Indicator (MBTI). More mainstream than the Enneagram, the MBTI is probably more familiar to some of you. For those who are new to the MBTI or need a refresher, it is another personality diagnostic aimed at helping you discover or at least formalize some of your core perceptions and decision-making tendencies. The MBTI is backboned by four dichotomies of cognitive function in which a single letter abbreviates each end of each dichotomy. The four dichotomies and their abbreviations are Introversion (I)–Extraversion (E), Sensing (S)–Intuition (N), Thinking (T)–Feeling (F), and Judging (J)–Perceiving (P). When participants complete the MBTI questionnaire, they are given a four-letter type that indicates their preferences within each of these four categories. There are 16 Myers-Briggs types in all. No type is better than the other.

When taken together, a person's preferences and thus their type can be revealing about their tendencies and overall personality. Based on Swiss psychiatrist Carl Jung's theories in his 1921 book *Psychological Types*, the questionnaire was developed by Isabel Briggs Myers and her mother, Katharine Briggs, during the World War II era to help first-time women workers determine which types of jobs would be most satisfying to them.[4] Though your choice set has thankfully progressed beyond the realm of riveting plane parts, typing telegraphs, and sewing military uniforms, we're optimistic that the MBTI has the potential to give you insight into work and a life that you find compelling.

About the Authors: Michael's MBTI Journey

I first took Myers-Briggs when I was in high school, my 10th-grade year, I think. I took it in a career planning class. After filling out more than 120 questions online, the site I was using told me I was an ENFJ. Much like opening an intriguing gift, I eagerly scrolled down the results page to discover the details behind my type abbreviation. As I read things like, "ENFJs are people-focused individuals. They live in a world full of people opportunities and love and have a knack for helping bring out the best in others . . ." I couldn't help but begin to nod in agreement. The words on the page were very consistent with how, at my core, I felt about the world. It was cool to read a nicely worded description of certain strong parts of my personality. Then I got to parts like, "ENFJs often define their lives based on others' needs, sometimes leading to self-neglect and eventual breakdown." At first, I remember feeling offended. I thought, "I'm not blind to my own needs, I mean, c'mon." But, after a little more honest reflection, I realized that those points were true too. Sometimes I did overextend myself; I definitely had my share of exhausted nights (and mornings for that matter).

The most powerful thing about my first encounter with Myers-Briggs was that it helped me think through some of the things that made me tick. It helped me see and acknowledge some of my most glaring strengths and weaknesses at that stage in my life. It provided formal warning of the hazards of being over-committed and stretched too thin in my relationships, but it also re-affirmed the inner sense that I wanted to help people, to affect their lives in a positive way. I had always felt a pull toward leadership, even from a young age, and the results of this first extensive self-diagnostic were incredibly empowering. The energy I gleaned from this first encounter helped me solidify my sense of self and encouraged me to continue the forays I had begun making into leadership at school. As I grew up, I eventually discovered organizations and groups—all comprised of great people—that really meant a lot to me, and I ended up pursuing active leadership roles within them. The work I do today leading and coaching students, entrepreneurs, and other professionals is due to the self-discovery process I started, in part, with Myers-Briggs.

Like the Enneagram, one of the most important things to keep in mind about the MBTI is that it is a basic diagnostic tool. It can be incredibly effective as a technique for starting your internal search and explanation, but by no means is it all-encompassing. In fact,

"Know yourself and you
will win all battles."

–Sun Tzu

it's basic accuracy and therefore usefulness is highly dependent on the state of the participant while taking the questionnaire. Honesty is obviously essential. So too is level-headedness and awareness. If, while you're filling out the questionnaire, you're gripped by your ego—as in you're caught up in a whirlwind of emotion, you're fixated on your story, or you're simply overanalyzing and manipulating the questions with your thoughts—you will arrive at results that are poor indicators of your fundamental perspectives and values. If, on the other hand, your are aware of the egoic ebb and flow within you and consciously try to put it aside, your results have the potential to be very insightful. Like the Enneagram, they can give you a strong indication of some of your core psychology. They too can provide you with a map for growth. You see, knowing your MBTI type should not be used as an excuse for negative or detrimental behavior. "It's okay that I neglect and over-stress myself because I'm ENFJ and that's what ENFJ's do," is an example of this excuse-making behavior and is a trap of most straight-forward personality-diagnosing techniques. Rather than lean on your type to justify some of your personal struggles, use it as a means to set improvement targets around these things. In this way, knowing your type gives you an opportunity to improve your weaknesses and the way you interact with the world around you, as well as giving you a solid place to start searching for the truest parts of you—a search that will lead to the discovery of your calling.

The Enneagram-MBTI Intersection

As you can see from our initial descriptions, the Enneagram and the MBTI are very closely related personality diagnostic tools. In order to bridge the two and to help you build some intuition around how one tool maps to the other, we wanted to give you a snapshot of how they are related. See Figure 11 for the Enneagram-MBTI correlative results of a research study done by Tom Flautt and John Richards in conjunction with the Association of Psychological Type.[5]

ENNEAGRAM TYPE	ASSOCIATED MBTI TYPE	ASSOCIATED PREFERENCES & TEMPERAMENTS
1 - Reformer	ISTJ, ESTJ	I, S, T, J, SJ
2 - Helper	ESFJ, ENFJ, ISFP, ESFP, ENFP, ISFJ	E, F
3 - Achiever	ENTJ, ENTP	E, T, NT
4 - Individualist	INFP, INFJ	I, N, F, P, NF
5 - Investigator	INTP, INTJ, ISTP, ISTJ	I, N, T, NT
6 - Loyalist	ISFJ, ISTJ	I, S, J, SJ
7 - Enthusiast	ESTP, ENTP, ENFP, ESFP	E, N, P
8 - Challenger	ESTJ, ENTJ	E, T, J
9 - Peacemaker	ISFP, INFP	I, F, P, SP

FIGURE 11

Beyond these correlative type relationships, we also wanted to give you a little bit of differentiable knowledge between the two tools. Here are the big picture differences:[6]

Enneagram:

- With only 9 types, it's easier to remember.
- It's newer to many professional settings and is therefore more novel—can sometimes offer a fresh perspective.
- Has a large emphasis on personal growth, development, and fulfillment.
- It explicitly showcases your healthy and unhealthy type.

MBTI:

- Rooted in traditional psychology (Jung).

- Well-developed applications. Commonly used in team building, management training, and leadership development. (Downside: very common, sometimes lacks novelty)

- Widely accepted by many counselors, coaches, consultants, and educators.

- People can tend to get stuck by their type label.

PEAKS AND VALLEYS

The next technique we'd like to give you is a fan favorite among our clients. It is a simple and direct reflection exercise that can be a powerful jumping off point for self-discovery. The technique is to think about and explore the best and worst times—or as we like to say, the peaks and valleys—in your life up to this point.

The purpose of this reflection isn't to mire you in the passionate joy or deflating doldrums of the past. Rather, it's to have you revisit your peaks and valleys with a learner's mindset. As you reflect upon the peak moments of your career, take note of what made them so special. Similarly, with the valleys, what contributed to them being so awful? Do the same thing with your personal life. What were the circumstances, attitudes, and events that led to your best moments? To your worst?

Genuine thoughtfulness is an important component of this method. It's easy to think back to a moment when you bought a new sports car and quickly label it a "peak" or a time when you lost an investment and say "valley." However, this technique is most useful when you explore your peaks and valleys in a deeply personal way. As we know from working with our myriad of clients, though our peak and valley indicators sometimes seem like they should be *when I got this* or *fell short of that* moments, they often are a lot more subtle. They often are much more internal. The challenge of this technique is to dig into the core of these moments and really find the essence of your past joy and meaning along with your past disappointment. When you do so, not only do you come to better understand the highs and lows you've experienced but you also learn more about the things that give you meaning. You learn more about the true you and the things that make you tick. Through examining the valleys, you're able to solidify the circumstances and moments that should be avoided, and by digging into the peaks, you can figure out what you really want more of going forward. On either side of the coin, you gain insight into the nature of your calling.

PEAK AND VALLEY: JEFF SMITH, CEO OF SANTA CLARA COUNTY

For the past three years, Behnam has worked with Santa Clara County and its visionary CEO, Jeff Smith. Jeff can trace his calling directly to a peak and valley he experienced early in his career. He regularly uses his closely linked best and worst moments to fuel his transformative work with Santa Clara County and to lead and inspire its fifteen thousand employees. His peak and valley in his words:

The biggest valley of my life and career occurred during the first year of my family practice medical residency. It was a perfect storm of sorts. I spent each day at the hospital stressed out, overworked, and consistently feeling that I was not good enough. A couple of my patients died during that first year and, even though I didn't do anything wrong, I felt an enormous amount of responsibility and guilt because of it. At home, things were choppy too. In order to do my residency, I had moved my wife and three-year-old son away from our Southern California friends and family support network and into the Northern California unknown. And she was pregnant again.

She was pregnant, had a three-year-old son, and I was constantly gone. Needless to say, it was not a good combination. In fact, it was lethal. Despite my best efforts, the marriage failed. My wife and I divorced and she moved away with the kids. I was absolutely crushed. Devastated. I roamed the halls of the hospital, often on autopilot, just trying to get through each day. I felt like an utter failure in every aspect of my life and slowly slipped into depression.

Several months later, right as I was hitting the deepest valley of my depression, something happened that would forever change the trajectory of my life. In order to make some extra money after the divorce, I had begun working in the psychiatric ward during my non-residency hours. It gave me something to do, kept me active, and gave me some added income. Plus, I felt quite at home being around other depressed people. One night, around eight o'clock, I was walking the psych ward halls and walked by a room where I saw a patient I had never seen before. The patient was an 18-year-old girl sitting completely still in a wheelchair. By some curious urge, I walked into the room and asked the nurses what was going on. They responded curtly saying, "You're not supposed to see this patient." Not satisfied with their answer, I decided to do a little digging. I soon found out that this girl (let's call her Jill) had actually been in the hospital for 9 months and that she suffered from catatonia—a condition associated with depression and schizophrenia where the body essentially turns off due to neurologic overload. That is to say, you're awake, alert, your personality is turned on, you can hear, you can think, but your body doesn't work. It's a rare and sometimes deadly disease.

As I was shunned out of the room, I found myself wondering, "Why aren't we doing something to treat her?" I was immediately overcome by the desire to investigate. I grabbed her chart and started digging. It turns out that Jill was scheduled to be transported two days later to a state psychiatric hospital to live out the rest of her days with catatonia. The prognosis was that she would probably die within a year. This decision had been made by the top administrator, the county mental health director, as the only option left for her. As I kept poring through her lengthy file, however, I found that this decision to give up on her had been made for political reasons, not medical reasons. Several of the prominent psychiatrists who had reviewed her case recommended that she be treated with electro-convulsive therapy (ECT), but the file showed that no ECT had been administered. It turns out that the county mental health director was philosophically against ECT so every time one of Jill's psychiatrists recommended it, he said "no" and moved on. And because state law required the county mental health director's approval on any ECT, the treatment was at a stalemate.

Looking at Jill's file and situation, I was overwhelmed with a desire to help. Though I didn't realize it then, my passion to help her recover was really an extension of my personal quest for recovery. By helping her fight hopelessness and negativity, maybe I could do the same for myself. I had to fight. I had to fight for the both of us. I had Jill transferred down to the medical ward where I was doing my residency. For the next two months, I labored with other doctors to reassess Jill's diagnosis and to arrange for ECT treatment. Knowing that I would need some political leverage to get the mental health director to approve the treatment, I carefully developed a relationship with his boss. I filled the boss in on the details of the situation and arranged for my attending supervisor, who was very respected by the boss, to explain the situation to him. The boss became convinced that ECT was an essential course of action.

Once I had his support, I went ahead and scheduled Jill for ECT. Three days before she was going to go, I called the mental health director asking for his official approval. He was none too happy that I had already scheduled the ECT procedure and proceeded to curse me out as the "idiot, know-nothing resident" that I was (by this point, I was used to this kind of treatment and was thus unaffected). I took this verbal lashing calmly and then reminded him in a not-so-subtle fashion that his boss thought that it was a good idea and that he should probably talk to him if he had any questions. After an angry hang-up and 30 minutes of waiting, he called back and said, "Bring the form over, you (expletive deleted)." I took it over and he signed it.

Three days later, Jill began her ECT treatment. She had it for three consecutive days. Though I attended the treatment with her the first two days in order to make certain that it was safe and humane, I couldn't make it to the third treatment because of a residency training meeting. After the meeting, I walked back to my unit with my attending physician, Sam (the one who had spoken to the boss). As we rounded the corner, we saw Jill standing at the nursing station and my jaw dropped. She turned to me and with a radiant smile said, "Hi, Dr. Smith." Speechless and flooded with joy, tears welled up in my eyes; I could not speak. Sam turned to me, looked me squarely in the eye, and said, "That's the closest thing I have ever seen to a miracle."

There, out of the depths of despair, came my peak. It is my high point. Every day since that moment has helped me frame my life. I realized deeply what a professor in medical school once told me: "When you care for a patient, you are caring for yourself, and all that you can offer that patient is yourself." Besides helping me to get out of my own depression, it taught me the value of persistence and doing the right thing. I learned to question authority and to hold fast to my basic values of caring, equity, justice, integrity, and empathy. No matter the challenge, there is always a way to work through it in a principled manner. The peak of my career has impressed upon me the value of tirelessly serving others and that, for the rest of my life, negativity and the constant "no" will not win out.

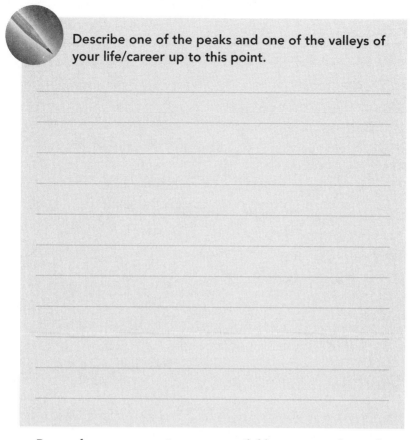

Describe one of the peaks and one of the valleys of your life/career up to this point.

Remember, our exercises are available at www.theinsideout effect.com as well.

WHOSE LINE IS IT ANYWAY?

We'd now like to look at a few more creative and dynamic forms of self-discovery. Many of you are probably familiar with the popular TV show *Whose Line Is It Anyway?* that aired on ABC during the late 1990s and early 2000s. As a quick refresher, it was a comedy show hosted by Drew Carey based on improvisational (improv) theatre. Over the course of each 30-minute program, the actors would improvise, as in create on the spot, a series of scenes and

> There's no point sitting here, using words that mean nothing. Go and experiment. It's time you got out of here. Go and re-conquer your kingdom, which has grown corrupt by routine. Stop repeating the same lesson, because you won't learn anything new that way."
>
> *–Paulo Coelho,* Aleph

comedic moments based on prompts from the host or the audience. To those of us watching, it seemed almost unbelievable that they could create such intricate—and more notably, hilarious—content off the top of their heads. There were certainly moments when we thought, *There's no way that wasn't scripted and rehearsed!* As it turns out, in addition to numerous hours of practice and, certainly, a heavy dose of cultivated talent, the improv actors on *Whose Line Is It Anyway?* were so successful because they subscribed to a fundamental improv principle called **"Yes, And . . ."**

In the improv world, "Yes, And . . ." means taking what your fellow actor does and building upon it. It's about *accepting offers* and building a story together. Though it may come as a surprise, this tenet of improv also has huge implications for self-discovery.

One of the biggest problems that plagues our ongoing sense of self is that we often become trapped in routine. And, with the exception of the small number of us fortunate enough to be living our calling, that routine is usually in some way mundane or, at the very least, self-limiting. It limits our daily experiences and therefore our daily learning about what types of activities, subjects, and opportunities resonate most with the true us. "Yes, And . . ." alleviates the negative symptoms of this routine. It let's us get out of our comfort zone. When, like Wayne Brady and the other improvisers on *Whose Line Is It Anyway?*, we say "Yes, And . . ." to life's offers, the world's possibilities open up before us. As legendary Stanford professor and founder of the Stanford Improvisers Patricia Madson writes in her book *Improv Wisdom*, "With the rule of yes, we call upon our capacity to envision, to create new and positive images. This yes invites us to find out what is right about the situation, what is good about the offer, what is worthy in the proposal."[7] It opens us up to the randomness and excitement of the world. When you say "yes" you agree to participate in an offer made by someone else, and when you say, "Yes, **AND** . . ." you agree to engage with and build upon that offer. This is our challenge to you. Start incorporating "Yes, And . . ." into your daily life. Say "yes" when your friend from college wants to go backpacking. When your wife wants to do a date night, respond with an excited "yes" and then say, ". . . and I'll make the reservation and plan the itinerary." As you say "Yes, And . . ." to more things, you begin having new and potentially eye-opening experiences. In addition to providing spontaneity, and often tons of fun, these experiences lead to incredible instances of self-discovery. You come to understand yourself on a deeper level, potentially discovering new likes, dislikes, and passions.

When was the last time you said "Yes, And . . ." to a brand new experience? How did it make you feel?

About the Authors: Behnam's "Yes, And . . ." Breakthrough

In the early 1990s, as I was getting toward the end of my PhD, I was a teaching assistant (TA) for a class on entrepreneurial finance. Up until that point, I had always had a big fear of speaking and presenting in class—probably because of my immigrant background and highly technical, engineering background. The class I was TA-ing was pretty dry and I managed to keep a low profile by being off to the side of the room during most sessions.

However, one day the professor was called away due to a family emergency. As he left, he informed me that I would be teaching the class the next day. I. Was. Petrified. Anytime I would raise my hand to speak in one of my classes, I felt like someone was jabbing me in the back. How on earth was I going to teach an entire class?!

After preparing nearly the entire night before, I went to class and delivered the lecture. To my surprise, with the exception of some initial nervousness, it went quite smoothly. In fact, it went well! After class, a bunch of students told me that it had been one of the most comfortable and intriguing lectures of the term, and that they really liked it.

My dad, who happened to be visiting at the time and whom, as you know from my story, I spent a lot of my youth trying to please, sat in on my lecture that day. I'll never forget, after the students left, he came up to me and said, "You should look at the left side of the room more." I immediately thought: Great, once again, I can't live up to his standard. However, he quickly and surprisingly continued, ". . . and you're a natural teacher." I was blown away. Not only had I enjoyed my first teaching experience, my dad thought I was a natural. At that moment, I discovered a new part of myself. I discovered that teaching is part of my calling. I heeded the feeling I got that day (as well as my dad's words) and I've been teaching ever since. It never would have happened if I didn't get out of my comfort zone and "Yes, And . . ." that first opportunity.

Practicing "Yes, And. . ." will get you out of your comfort zone and into the realm of new discovery and possibility. It'll take you to where the magic happens.

Frequently, our frustration with identifying our calling comes from a limited perspective. Of what we've seen and experienced, we've identified things we like, but *what is it that we love?* Steve Jobs, one of the most innovative business leaders of our time once discussed "Yes, And . . ." in the context of people's careers. He said, "Your work is going to fill a large part of your life, and the only way to be truly satisfied is to do what you believe is great work. And the only way to do great work is to love what you do. If you haven't found it yet, keep looking and don't settle. As with all matters of

> It is impossible to live without failing at something, unless you live so cautiously that you might as well not have lived at all—in which case you fail by default."
>
> –J.K. Rowling

the heart, you'll know when you find it."[8] Many of us, either in our professional or personal lives, have yet to find it. To aid us in our attempt to do so, we should strive to experience more. Put yourself in situations outside of your routine. Accept your friend's offer to go swing dancing next Friday. Say "yes" when your new co-worker asks for a ride home. You never know what opportunities and self-learning might present itself to you.

Of course, like everything we've discussed so far, this is a technique for self-discovery, not a rule of law that should be followed every moment of every day. Don't ignore the fundamentals of your daily life—don't forget to feed the kids because you accepted an offer to go to an evening wine tasting class! Rather, just start incorporating "Yes, And . . ." when you can. Don't mistake this for us letting you off the hook because the reality is that you can say "Yes, And . . ." *far more often* than you currently do. Use it to break up your routine. Use it to open yourself to new experiences. Use it, like the incredible cast of *Whose Line Is It Anyway?*, to craft wacky, fun, and unbelievable stories that teach you more about yourself, what you like and, over time, perhaps help you illuminate your calling.

JOURNALING

Just as "Yes, And . . ." is a continuous and daily method of self-discovery, so too is journaling. Journaling is a daily or every-few-days or weekly check-in with yourself in which you have an opportunity to sit down with pen and paper or your computer and introspect. This introspection is about honest truth seeking. It gives you an opportunity to search for moments of personal meaning and fulfillment.

Now, we're fully aware that the term "journaling" connotes different things for different people—not all of them enticing. For us, the 1990s movie *Harriet the Spy* comes to mind for some reason. For others, an image of your sister hiding a pink-bound notebook under her pillow is probably more along the lines of what "journaling" evokes. Either way, if you hold any negative or pre-pubescent reticence toward journaling, we urge you to stick with us and give it a shot.

The best thing about journaling is that it creates a physical record of your state of mind, your feelings, and your core perspectives over time—things that you might otherwise forget. After a while, this record can reveal interesting insights into your perspectives and pattern of feeling in certain situations. And, of course, these insights are the essence of the self-discovery process. As with the Enneagram or Myers-Briggs, we ask that you try to approach journaling with an honest and aware mindset. The journaling we're talking about is not the egoic pining "I hate Billy because he has a cooler lunch box" content of your elementary school journal (or the present-day equivalent, "I really resent Ana for getting that promotion"), but rather is aimed at getting in touch with the core you (i.e., if you start by writing about your resentment toward Ana, make a concerted effort to explore *why* you resent her—dig deeper).

What this method looks like for you can take many forms. For some, an extended daily entry detailing the nuances of the day's events and how they were personally affected is the obvious choice. However, there are many other ways to go about it. We are fond of just writing down "notable moments" as they occur every few days. Our entries are short and to the point. They often focus around what did or didn't surprise us about the way we reacted to a certain situation. In this way, we explicitly write from a perspective of personal understanding.

Our favorite approach to journaling is what we call gratitude journaling. Gratitude journaling is simple: All you have to do is write down five things you're grateful for every couple of days. Whether you write down a relationship, a recent conversation, a beautiful skyline, a piece of knowledge, or something else, it's all good. The writing itself is straightforward—you just need one sentence or a bulleted list. The content requires a little more thought, especially over time, but it's not too difficult either. And the great thing is that the results can be profound. People who write down what they're grateful for cultivate their self-awareness by formally figuring out what they value and hold most highly. They also become happier and less stressed. A study done by Robert Emmons at UC-Davis and Michael McCullough at the University of Miami showed that people who kept a gratitude journal just once a week for two months were more optimistic, happier, healthier, and worked out more often than those who did not. Beyond that, they've also found that people who keep gratitude journals are less anxious, fall asleep faster, sleep longer, and wake up more refreshed.[9] As a result of his research, Dr. Emmons says, "If you want to sleep more soundly, count blessings, not sheep."[10]

Regardless of how you choose to go about it, simply writing down your state of mind and the things you're grateful for can be extremely useful on your journey toward greater self-discovery and, as you can see, overall well-being. As much as we think we know what we like and dislike, what lights us up and what turns us off, there is usually a lot of subtlety in between. The reality is that we usually don't take the time to formally reflect on and explore it.

Even if you're one who does reflect more often, you probably don't remember it all. Written reflection helps you do that.

However you choose to implement this method, make sure you do it in a way that fits with your lifestyle. As we'll explore in earnest in BE, change, even little things, can be hard. Set yourself up for success with this method by choosing a writing routine that jives with you. If, for example, you're a first-time journaler, reflect on your week and reflect on your weekend—as in, write something every Friday and every Sunday night. Build this routine into a habit, adding more frequent entries if you feel compelled to do so. Finding writing intervals that work for you will keep journaling from becoming a chore—something that will surely lead to you resenting the process rather than enjoying a journey of self-learning. And, ultimately, keep your eyes on the bigger picture. Journaling is not about laboriously crafting elegant memoirs; it is about paying attention to and noting the truths about your core self. *It's about understanding your moments of meaning and happiness.* Write that italicized line on the cover of your notebook or as the header on your Word document. It'll help turn this technique into something meaningful and lasting.

MEDITATION AND MINDFULNESS

Our next method for self-discovery is particularly noteworthy. It's noteworthy because, in addition to being an incredibly effective tool for self-discovery, it is a powerful tool for greater personal purpose and happiness. It also, on a more cautionary note, tends to be one of the more difficult and controversial techniques that we talk about. The method is, in a general term, meditation.

The word "meditation," like the word "journaling," evokes a number of reactions across a large spectrum of people. For many of us in the Western world, "meditation" immediately

> Look at your feet. You are standing in the sky. When we think of the sky, we tend to look up, but the sky actually begins at the earth. We walk through it, yell into it, rake leaves, wash the dog, and drive cars in it. We breathe it deep within us. With every breath, we inhale millions of molecules of sky, heat them briefly, and then exhale them back into the world."
>
> –Diane Ackerman

conjures an image of a cross-legged, eyes-closed Buddha contemplating the sound of still air. In other words, it conjures up a highly foreign, strange, and generally unrelatable picture. Herein lies the difficulty and controversy. Very similar to the stigma we talked about earlier around honestly exploring the question *who am I?*, many of us carry strong judgments regarding meditation. Like many of our excuses about avoiding self-exploration and discovery, we claim that meditation just doesn't fit into the realm of our driven, pragmatic lifestyles. However, like before, a lot of our rejection stems from fears about cultural and personal acceptance. So, for those of you currently thinking thoughts like "hippie B.S." or "weird yoga stuff," just stick with us. Remember, those thoughts are not you. They are your egoic mind jumping in and trying to influence you. It knows that meditation has the potential to bring you further awareness, which diminishes its control over the way you see the world. Your harsh judgments, if you have any, are your ego trying to survive. As we go through meditation techniques you'll see that, though certain applications of this method end up being very similar to that image of Buddha, the large majority of them are much simpler and more comfortable.

To begin alleviating any potential discomfort created by the stereotypical images of meditation that we're all used to, allow us to begin by demystifying meditation and defining it in our own terms. The way *we* view and define meditation is: any act that focuses the mind inward and to the present moment, often characterized by an increased focus on breathing and stillness. Simple, straightforward. With that definition, each of you could spend five minutes brainstorming activities or times of the day where you could easily meditate. In fact, with that definition, you all could probably identify moments where you already meditate. For instance, think about the last time you were really exasperated with a situation. As you worked through all the details, you might have had a moment where, together with a large, up-and-down shoulder movement, you let out a heavy sigh. We're sure all of you can recall such a moment. Though you probably didn't know it then, your body was naturally combating stress and anxiety by engaging in a mini-mediation—a moment where you attempted to let go of the external weight you were carrying through a deep, resounding breath. You see, you've already got a head start.

Some of our favorite meditative practices are those that can be done on the go and fit into our busy lifestyles. Many of these methods are what our good friend and author of *Positive Intelligence,* Shirzad Chamine, calls Positive Intelligence Quotient (PQ) Reps. In his words, PQ Reps are quick, three-breath actions that help develop your sense of curiosity, peace, calmness, joy, and creativity. Among many other things, he counts wiggling your toes attentively, noticing your butt on your chair, feeling your fingerprint ridges by rubbing your fingers together, and truly *seeing* the person in front of you as PQ Rep mini-meditations that help you balance your mind, increase your awareness, and work toward discovering further personal truth.[11]

About the Authors: Michael's Meditation Journey

My first experience with meditation (or so I thought at the time) happened several years ago when a good friend of mine encouraged me to take a wellness and meditation class he was involved in teaching. Though the course sounded pleasant—he described it as helping people increase the sense of balance, peace, and self-awareness in their lives—I was pretty lukewarm about taking it because of the mediation component. Truth-be-told, it took my friend a year of encouragement to get me to take the class.

On the first day of the course, I walked into a small, wood-floored room covered in brightly colored yoga mats. I remember thinking, "Oh, no! This is going to be so awkward. What have I gotten myself into?" After introducing myself to a few of the other people around me, my friend and his co-instructor walked in and got things started. Rather than tossing me and the rest of the class directly into the yoga-meditation fire, they started with a friendly, disarming, and, to my surprise, very grounded conversation about why we had all come to this course and what they hoped to give us. They explained that we spend so much of our lives filling our mind with knowledge and information without ever really taking the time to understand how our mind works. They laid a roadmap for the week ahead, saying that we'd spend a lot of time in conversation, playing games, breathing, and yes, meditating. As if they anticipated the squeamishness going on inside of some of us, they reassured the whole class that we weren't there for some abstract walk through la-la land. We were there to learn from one another as well as through a set of pragmatic techniques how to better understand our constantly ticking minds. Through this understanding, they said, we could better appreciate the good things in our lives, be less vexed by the bad things, work more efficiently, and, above all, find more happiness and meaning in everything we did.

As the course got underway, I realized that my initial reservations were completely unfounded. We spent a lot of time in interesting conversation, digging away at the things that consistently undermined our well-being. When we got to the actual meditation, it wasn't bad at all. Our instructors, my friend included, were great about calling out the potential awkwardness some of us felt about it and laughing with us at the things that initially seemed strange and awkward. I had expected it to be pretty useless, but I was so wrong. Sitting there with my eyes closed and my attention turned inward was incredible. It was as if I was able to dial down the volume of the world around me and just focus on myself for a little while. There was something so soothing about sitting in a room listening to the calm, collective inhale and exhale of everyone sitting around me. It was as if we were all concentrating on a calm truth at the same time. We were all striving for deeper self-awareness together. Despite my initial reservations, I had to admit it was pretty centering.

In the couple of years that have passed since I took the class, I cannot claim that I am an obsessive meditator. I am neither the world's most centered man nor its most self-aware person. I am, however, a once skeptic who has come to appreciate the role meditation can play in self-discovery and happiness boosting. And, as we talk about in this book, I've realized that meditation comes in many shapes and sizes. Whether it's taking an extra moment to breathe and stretch in bed when I wake up in the morning or it's taking a timeout from writing emails to turn my attention back inward, I find little moments of meditation all over the place. In fact, since taking the class, I've realized that I meditated long before my formal introduction. It turns out that I've been meditating since I started playing the guitar over seven years ago. For a long time, I always noticed that playing a guitar was cathartic for me. I would routinely lose my worries and stresses in the notes and just play. I would play at the end of a long day, or in the middle of doing work. It always energized and calmed me simultaneously. After realizing that meditation is any activity that turns your attention inward and into the present moment, I recognized that guitar playing is simultaneously one of my favorite hobbies and most powerful forms of meditation. It's uplifting and, though I didn't always realize it, brings me into stronger self-awareness.

As you can see, meditation and mindfulness can take countless forms. For some it's a deliberate 20- to 30-minute respite of concentrated breathing every day; for others it's something done sitting in traffic, going to the bathroom, walking down a hallway, or taking a shower. We recommend you try whatever technique you feel has the best potential for you. You might start by simply being in concentrated silence for the first 5 minutes after waking up for the next few days, focusing solely on your breath. Or maybe try to do 100 PQ Reps a day for the next week. In fact, Shirzad loves the effects of PQ Reps so much that he guarantees everyone he works with that if they begin doing 100 PQ Reps a day, they will have someone in their life (someone who knows them well but doesn't know they've started the PQ Rep process) come up to them and say something about how they've changed. They'll either comment on how grounded you seem or how even-keeled you've been acting lately. They might even ask if you've been on a relaxing vacation or trip recently.

Meditation, whether it be jamming on your guitar, going on centering evening walks, sitting eyes-closed on your bedroom floor, or doing PQ Reps, works. We know this from personal experience. Both in our own lives and in the lives of numerous others, we've been able to witness the effectiveness of meditation in helping increase self-awareness, mindfulness, and happiness. We also know this from countless studies that have been conducted on meditation's effects on our physical and mental well-being. Over the last four decades, thousands of studies at hundreds of universities have showcased multiple positive benefits of meditation. It decreases stress, anxiety, and fear, while increasing joy and self-awareness. Meditation has been linked to stabilizing blood pressure,[12] lowering heart and respiratory rates,[13] and strengthening the immune system.[14] Give meditation a try. The positive effects it has on your health, along with the insights it gives you into your core self, can be truly surprising.

Brain Bite: Meditation
Brain Breathing

Not only has meditation been linked to positive health and emotions, it has also been connected to structural changes in the brain. Researchers at Harvard Medical School and Massachusetts General Hospital have recently discovered that meditation leads to increases in gray-matter density in the hippocampus, posterior cingulate, and the temporoparietal junction—areas of the brain associated with empathy, learning, stress-regulation, self-awareness, and memory.[15] Who knew that dedicated time turned inward could have such a significant impact on our brain's ability to learn, connect with others, and regulate stress? Regular meditation has the potential to help you enhance the meaningful connections and relationships in your life as well as be happier and more contented.

AUTHENTIC FEEDBACK AND
THE JOHARI WINDOW

Our last method for self-exploration is authentic feedback. Authentic feedback is our umbrella term for any technique or process that involves asking others about who they perceive you to be. It can be an interesting and useful way to discover things about yourself that you have a hard time seeing when you look within. It also can reveal inconsistencies between who you are and how you act because, of course, when you ask the audience around you about you, they are going to be basing their responses on what they've observed, on the external actions you've taken. This fundamental nature of the feedback process makes it a powerful, two-way tool for self-awareness. Through it, you can simultaneously learn new things about the core you as well as discover actions that don't resonate at all with who you perceive yourself to be, actions that you can then modify to live and work in greater self-alignment, happiness, and effectiveness.

Emerging from the work we've done with executives and Stanford MBAs, one of our favorite frames of reference for the self-awareness that is cultivated through authentic feedback is called the Johari Window. Created by Joseph Luft and Harry Ingham in the 1950s, the Johari Window shows how, through feedback and honest dialogue with others, an individual is able to expand the "public area" of personal awareness.[16] In Figure 12, we show the half of the Johari Window that is directly connected to someone getting useful feedback on his "blind areas." As the feedback process goes on, his blind area reduces and his open awareness expands. Through authentic feedback and a model like the Johari Window, an individual can become more known—both to others and, most importantly, to her- or himself.

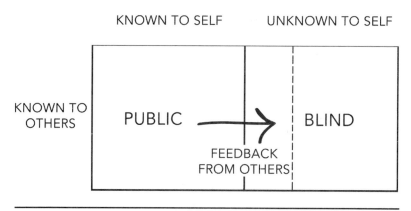

FIGURE 12

When done right, authentic feedback can be very powerful in a professional setting. It can have huge consequences on people's levels of self-awareness, the meaning they find in their work, and the effort they put in on a daily basis. Gary Knepp, an executive at a start-up company from the Northwest, had this to say about the power of utilizing authentic feedback in the self-discovery process:

As with many early-stage companies, the day-to-day pressures of revenue, staffing, cash flow, and client management frequently displace our longer-range team and individual development objectives. However, we recently set aside a day to catch up on those things by having our entire team engage in an authentic feedback process.

Kicked off by having the whole team take a basic workplace personality assessment, our team development day then quickly proceeded to authentic feedback. Each member of our team presented the results of their assessment, which the rest of us then used as the catalyst for giving them feedback. In my case, the assessment essentially said that I am a driven, goal-oriented, type A personality who likes having a large degree of input and control on the projects I work on with a particular focus on the "so what?" ROI question. Using this as a starting point, my colleagues began chiming in with their take. Many of them resoundingly echoed my assessment results saying that that is how I often showed up in the work environment. Several people expressed appreciation for my strategic business mind and perpetual focus on how we were allocating our resources. However, others pointed out that while these characteristics were helpful for a large portion of my work—things like hitting revenue milestones, achieving valuation objectives for future financing initiatives, and weighing important trade-offs on partnering decisions—they sometimes undermined my relationships. Several employees noted that some of these traits appeared to be at the root of my semi-frequent frustration and head-butting with our CEO. A few even mentioned that they had felt intimidated and unable to be heard by me in certain moments, that I had just steam-rolled them out of conversations. It was sobering and useful feedback. Though I never really saw myself that way, as I heard their words and firsthand stories, I could definitely see what they were talking about. As they spoke, I found myself feeling really grateful that they were able to share so candidly with me.

*Through our authentic feedback process, my co-workers and I all learned about ourselves in new ways. Some of the feedback reinforced things about myself that I like and other bits illuminated things I want to work on. In either case, setting aside a day to openly and directly **talk to one another about one another** was a powerful thing. It helped us learn as individuals, as well as improve as a company. The feedback we exchanged helped us with our personal development, job function, and role as a positive* *contributor to our team dynamic. It left a large impact on me and is something I plan to continue doing periodically in the future.*

As you can see, both from Gary's experience and the feedback you can just imagine getting from your peers, the authentic feedback process can be a powerful tool for realizing how you actually *act* day to day. This realization has strong implications for your self-awareness. It allows you to recognize alignments—or misalignments—between who you are and who you appear to be, therefore sharpening your sense of self.

Feedback processes can take a wide number of forms. In a work setting, they are often administered by the human resources team or by outside consultants like at Gary's company. In your personal life, they can be as simple as having an earnest conversation with someone you trust and who knows you well. In fact, some people who embark on serious personal change efforts explicitly form a change support group that holds them accountable, acts as a sounding board, and offers encouragement along the way. Whether you've intentionally done this or not, asking for feedback from a group of people you trust can be an effective way to get accurate, honest, and meaningful feedback. Have them write you letters. Have a 30-minute phone call with each of them asking for sincere feedback. Heck, have them over for dinner and talk together about what it is you're trying to learn, accomplish, and change, and ask them for their help.

Now, we realize that the authentic feedback technique has the potential to yield a variety of results when it comes to substantive self-learning and awareness. The reality is that some of the people whom you ask for feedback are going to give unhelpful responses. Perhaps a person you ask won't know you well enough, or sometimes even more unhelpfully, they'll know you really well in only one or two contexts. Either way, there's always the potential to get limited or incomplete views when you try to collect informative and useful opinions from those who know you. To avoid these pitfalls and, in our opinion, sidestep the greatest frustrations that can result from a hackneyed feedback process, it's imperative that you spend time on setting the *context* of the feedback. Tell the person or people you're asking for feedback the reason why you're asking. Tell them that negative feedback is okay, as long as it's honest and constructive (this should never just be a bashing session). Reassure them that you're coming from a place of openness and self-learning and that you're not going to be hyper-sensitive to the things they say—after all, you're getting feedback on how you *act* and those actions might or might not be in line with who you are. This is a litmus test, an ask-the-audience check-in for personal consistency. Encourage them to be thoughtful and specific because that's when your learning will take place. If you do these things, if you take the time to set the context, you will maximize your chance of having a relevant and useful feedback experience that results in increased self-awareness. And remember, as for your part, stay open to negative feedback and ready to admit to areas for improvement. Don't be this guy:

About the Authors: Behnam's First Feedback Process

My first job after getting my Masters in Electrical Engineering was at IBM. On my first day of work, I realized that everyone on my team referred to my boss as "The Devil." After a few weeks of work, I understood why he had garnered this nickname—he was a micromanager and a conflict-starter. Constantly tearing down the people on my team, he would only change his tune for a few weeks every year around management review time (an IBM HR practice). A buddy of mine and I decided not to cower under his yearly façade of kindness and gave him our honest low mark feedback. A week after the reviews were all in, he pulled the whole team into a small conference room and put the negative feedback we had given up on the overhead projector and demanded to know who had given him such poor reviews. He stared around the room intently for almost three silent minutes, daring the two of us to come forward. My friend and I never did, but it was a lesson in terrible management that has stayed with me throughout my career and served as a constant reminder to try to be open to feedback, no matter how difficult. In fact, his example was one of the biggest motivators for me to go back to school and get my PhD in Management. Though it may seem surprising, I'll forever be grateful for him.

Don't be The Devil. The Devil completely undermined his team's feedback process because he failed to set the context required for peer feedback to be successful. He didn't have the right attitude, he wasn't open, and, clearly, he had no intention of actually learning about himself through the process. Blowing up and going on a witch hunt based on non-flattering feedback will not only alienate those giving feedback but also signifies that you have missed the opportunity for self-learning and understanding. When it comes to peer feedback, be Gary, not The Devil.

Actions Speak Louder Than Words

Now that we've talked at length about self-discovery, about honing in on your calling, it's time to act. Simply reading the words on the preceding pages will not increase your self-awareness or bring you closer to greater fulfillment and personal performance. You must actively engage with them in order to grow and learn.

Please, do not turn to and begin reading the next section until you've had some time to begin the self-exploration presented in these past two chapters. In the time that you take, please spend at least 30 minutes a day on intentional self-exploration. Write it on your To-Do list, put it on your calendar, or set a reminder alarm on your phone. Do 50 PQ Reps a day, begin keeping a gratitude journal, find out your Enneagram number, and "Yes, And . . ." a few new experiences. Pick a handful of the techniques we discussed and try them out. As you go, slowly put the things you discover into the SEE framework. List new strengths. Write about things that evoke deep meaning and give you elated joy.

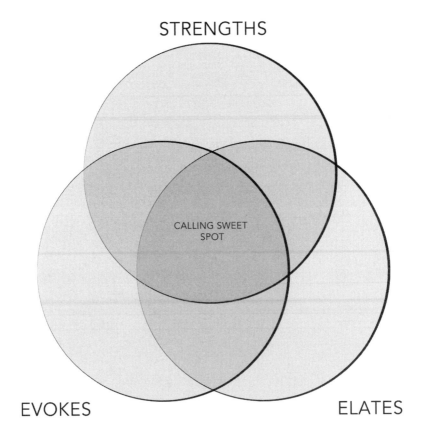

STRENGTHS

CALLING SWEET
SPOT

EVOKES

ELATES

When you feel like you've made some progress, proceed to the next section. The usefulness of what comes next is highly contingent on your recent, active engagement with the question: *What, at my core, makes me tick?* It depends on an active striving for greater self-understanding and awareness. Take the time to grapple with these hard topics for a while. Then, when you feel like you're more self-connected and a little more self-aware, come on back.

Keep in mind, this is just one iteration toward greater self-knowledge. Don't pressure yourself to be the most-enlightened version of you or have a finalized version of SEE before you proceed. Just strive to be more in touch with the core you than you are right now. The reality is that we are dynamic beings and self-awareness is a continuous process. For a few, the parameters and details of your calling may be lurking just beneath the surface and will be clearly revealed with just a little bit of introspection. For many others, the specifics of your calling are much more obscured. You might have a general sense of it (which is fantastic), but the particulars are hazy. That's absolutely fine. As you go through these techniques not only right now but in the weeks and months ahead, you will slowly add clarity. As you "Yes, And . . ." more experiences, you'll learn. As you gain momentum on a gratitude journal, you'll gain insight. As you ask trusted peers for feedback, you'll see more clearly. Set a little time aside and take this first step with us now. As time goes on, remind yourself to continue to KNOW yourself better. Tape a note to your mirror or set a reminder on your phone, and keep pushing. You're on the doorstep of increasing your sense of fulfillment and peak performance level. You're on the doorstep of clarifying your calling.

THE TOOLS
A SUMMARY

- This chapter is all about the formal exploration of *who you are.*

- We use the **SEE: S**trengths–**E**vokes–**E**lates Venn diagram as an organizing tool for the exploration and learning done throughout the "Exploring You" process.

- Self-exploration is not a uniform science. Try different techniques and see what works for you. Be open to continuously trying new things over time.

- Personality diagnostics such as the Enneagram and the Myers-Briggs Type Indicator often serve as good starting points for self-discovery.

- Take time to reflect on the Peaks and Valleys (or the Highs and Lows) of your life. With thoughtful introspection, these moments can be incredibly revealing about who you are and what matters most.

- Practice saying "Yes, And . . ." to new opportunities. You'll learn a lot about yourself and probably have a good time too!

- Journal, express gratitude, and record what you find meaningful and what makes you happy.

- Meditate. It's good for your health, happiness, and your brain.

- Seek feedback as a way to cultivate your self-awareness. Make sure you set the context.

NATE'S STATUS UPDATE

Worn-out, unfulfilled, and underperforming, Nate agreed that trying to live closer to his calling, trying to be more in alignment with his values and core self, could be a helpful step in him becoming happier and more effective. He decided to give the Inside-Out Effect a shot and agreed to start going through KNOW-BE-LEAD.

As with all of our clients, Nate's first step was to take a look at who he was not. He had to take the initial steps toward cleaning out the poop in his fish tank and begin to disassociate from his strongest identity pitfalls. After some lengthy conversation, Nate landed on two major identity pitfalls that were really clouding his fish tank. The first was his long-standing "what's next?" approach to success. He realized that the majority of the time that perspective represented an attachment to his appearance. "What's next?" was really a perspective aimed at increases in status or material wealth. When Nate put his sense of well-being and effectiveness in the "what's next?" realm, he was continually placing his self-worth in the type of car he drove, the amount of jewelry Chloe had, the size of their home, and the number of vacations they could take. As Nate said when we first spoke to him, he has slowly realized that his "what's next" orientation is leaving him with a sense of emptiness. "In fact," he said, "I now realize it is a poisonous and chronically unfulfilling way to live. I need to let go of that perspective. Let go of that story." The other major pitfall plaguing Nate was the nasty story-thought-emotion web he was holding onto about his leadership at work. Through a little conversation, he realized that he was in fact conflating the *what's happening* with the *spin* his thoughts were telling him. With some coaching Nate was able to undo the tangled misidentification he was doing via the story he was telling himself:

His mistake:

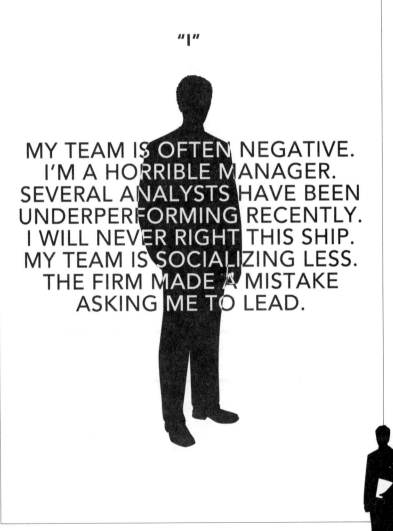

"I"

MY TEAM IS OFTEN NEGATIVE.
I'M A HORRIBLE MANAGER.
SEVERAL ANALYSTS HAVE BEEN
UNDERPERFORMING RECENTLY.
I WILL NEVER RIGHT THIS SHIP.
MY TEAM IS SOCIALIZING LESS.
THE FIRM MADE A MISTAKE
ASKING ME TO LEAD.

The reality:

WHAT WAS HAPPENING: HIS STORY:

MY TEAM IS OFTEN NEGATIVE.   I'M A HORRIBLE MANAGER.
SEVERAL ANALYSTS HAVE BEEN   I WILL NEVER RIGHT THIS SHIP.
UNDERPERFORMING RECENTLY.   THE FIRM MADE A MISTAKE
MY TEAM IS SOCIALIZING LESS.   ASKING ME TO LEAD.

After Nate came into some initial awareness around two of the major identity pitfalls that he routinely succumbed to, we asked him to mentally empty those stories and thoughts from his fish tank. He pictured clear water and unmarred opportunity all around him. He then ventured into self-discovery. Though Nate had a lot of intuitions about who he was and what was most important in his life, he willingly undertook some formal self-exploration in order to calm the storm brewing within him and really vet the fundamental assumptions he had about his life. Given his busy and self-described "pragmatic" lifestyle, he chose to focus inwardly using the following four relatively flexible KNOW techniques: the Enneagram, a daily gratitude journal, PQ Reps, and authentic feedback.

On the very first day, Nate sat down and took the Enneagram QUEST. After completing the questionnaire, he discovered that he was a Five—an Investigator. (This happened to be consistent with the INTJ Myers-Briggs typology he had scored several years earlier.) As he read through the type description, though there were a few lines that didn't immediately resonate with him, he saw a lot of himself within the words on the page. Several lines in particular really stuck out: "Fives are alert, insightful, and curious. They are able to concentrate and focus on developing complex ideas, skills, and strategies . . . Fives want to find out why things are the way they are . . . They are always searching, asking questions, and delving into things in depth . . . Fives often have leadership skills and intellect, but they usually choose to remain in the background until they see a real need to take over the lead."[17] Nate couldn't help but recognize just how accurately these words seemed to describe his core perspective. As he began to analyze his life, he realized just how much he enjoys strategic planning and analytics. *It's no wonder I ended up staying with the firm so long,* he thought, *something about the long-term policy strategy work that we do just really seems to click with me.* He also really resonated with the Five's leadership description. He remembered back to when he was first promoted to a management position over five years ago. He felt unsure about his ability to take over for the team lead that had come before him. He remembered thinking, *Linda, the woman before me, is so competent. Why do I need to take over?* Now, in light of his current team problems, Nate read and thought for a while about the lines "Other people may have a difficult time understanding Fives. Often consumed in thought, Fives may come off as aloof, reserved, or detached . . . Their focused attention unwittingly serves to distract them from their most pressing practical problems . . . The challenge to Fives is to understand that they can pursue whatever questions or problems spark their imaginations *and* maintain relationships."[18] Though he'd have to do more digging, Nate found these notes on how other people might sometimes see Fives as very useful starting points for beginning to think about some of the cohesion problems that had been affecting his team at work lately.

After our first few meetings with Nate, he conceded that he didn't feel like a ritual of regular and extended journaling would ultimately be successful given his lukewarm attitude toward free-writing and his time-pressed lifestyle. Instead, he committed to keeping a daily gratitude journal. Every night before going to bed, he began taking a few minutes to list five things in his life or about his day for which he was grateful. They could be simple and direct, but they needed to be sources of true gratitude. Common inclusions were Chloe and the kids, as well as their house and lifestyle. However, after a handful of days, Nate found himself getting more specific and enjoying the process more and more. For example, on day one, he wrote "Chloe" on his list. A week later, the entry was "A loving wife, Chloe, who, unlike many of my colleagues' wives, often makes me a delicious lunch to take to work in the morning." As Nate began to write down more detailed answers, he slowly found himself growing more in touch with some of his core values and perspectives, and, in turn, the source of his happiness and motivation.

In addition to keeping a daily gratitude journal, Nate committed to trying to do 75 PQ Reps a day. His favorites included attentively wiggling his toes whenever he sat down at his desk, truly feeling the texture of the steering wheel as he drove home in traffic, and trying to sense every drop of water on his body while he showered or washed his hands and face. As *Positive Intelligence* author Shirzad encourages, Nate took three deep breaths and focused on the PQ rep at hand every time he did a rep. He began to find the reps very centering and saw them as great ways to bring his mind back to a positive and present place throughout the day.

Last and slightly more involved, Nate asked some of the key players in his life to fill out a simple feedback form. On it he included questions such as "How do I act when I'm at my best?" and "How do I act when I'm at my worst?" "These days—meaning the last 6–12 months—where do I fall on the Worst-to-Best-Self Scale (1 being worst, 10 being best)?" Nate gave the form to the members of his team at work, two of the VPs he worked with regularly, his wife, and a few close friends. He emphasized that he wanted their constructive but also honest feedback. He briefly explained the concept of the Johari Window and how authentic feedback was really a way to learn about his blind areas and grow in self-awareness. He reassured them that he wouldn't be offended if they listed some of his shortcomings or "things to improve on." In fact, he said, he was extra curious about that type of feedback. After giving everyone a handful of days to fill out the form, he collected them and took a look. Consistent with some of his general feelings at work and at home, both Chloe and his team members expressed some concern about how attentive and engaged he has been lately. To summarize, his team noted how closed to feedback and generally disinterested he has seemed of late, while his wife mentioned just how deflated and generally un-affectionate he has been in the last handful of months. Nearly everyone who took the survey noted that he's not been his best self recently. After taking another look at his Five Enneagram type, Nate began to see a few consistencies that didn't justify, but at least helped explain, his rigidness and detachment over the recent period in which his overall satisfaction and sense of purpose had been lagging.

After committing to doing these exercises, Nate began feeling better slowly but surely. After just three weeks, he felt more positive; he felt like he was beginning to see himself in a more honest light; and, to his surprise, he even noticed a subtle change in the energy he began bringing to the office. As he stuck with it, he began to alight upon his core values and better understand the nature of his calling. After three weeks of doing his KNOW techniques, Nate's SEE model began to overflow with personal insights (check out the following simplified version). Nate's committed use of his chosen techniques began to bring him a greater sense of self-awareness and, even more powerfully, hope.

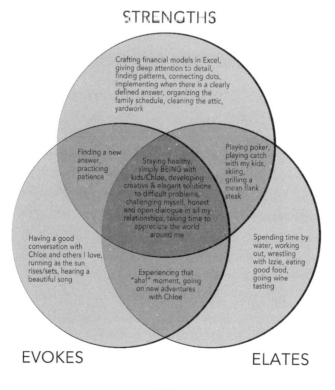

STRENGTHS

Crafting financial models in Excel, giving deep attention to detail, finding patterns, connecting dots, implementing when there is a clearly defined answer, organizing the family schedule, cleaning the attic, yardwork

Finding a new answer, practicing patience

Staying healthy, simply BEING with kids/Chloe, developing creative & elegant solutions to difficult problems, challenging myself, honest and open dialogue in all my relationships, taking time to appreciate the world around me

Playing poker, playing catch with my kids, skiing, grilling a mean flank steak

Having a good conversation with Chloe and others I love, running as the sun rises/sets, hearing a beautiful song

Experiencing that "aha!" moment, going on new adventures with Chloe

Spending time by water, working out, wrestling with Izzie, eating good food, going wine tasting

EVOKES

ELATES

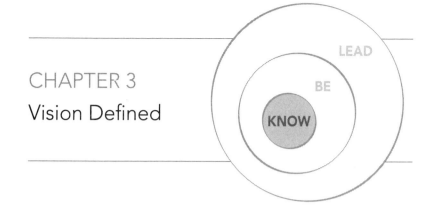

CHAPTER 3
Vision Defined

Welcome back! We hope you took at least several days to try out some of the techniques presented in the last two chapters. Hopefully the time you spent was revealing and productive, and by now you're feeling more balanced and self-aware. You're getting a little better at identifying and disassociating from your ego. You're feeling more conscious. Though you might not have the details of your calling pinned down exactly, you should have a much better understanding of it than you did when we started this journey. The answers to questions like: What makes me tick? What am I passionate about? What types of things give me meaning? and What do I value most? should be more readily accessible and honest than they have been in the past. If you feel like you can pretty confidently generate answers to these types of questions—answers that are, at least given where you currently stand, enduring and true—you're ready to take the next step. If for some reason you feel like you're not to the point of honestly and confidently answering these types of questions, that's completely fine. We recommend that you spend a little more time with the methods in the previous chapters. Successfully defining your calling is contingent upon having a strong sense of your true self, so keep pushing until that's the case for you. Go back and keep digging. No need to rush or pressure yourself, just take the

> It is a terrible thing to see and have no vision."
>
> *–Helen Keller*

time you need. We'll be waiting for you when you feel ready.

This chapter is about bringing it all together. It's about taking the work you've done throughout KNOW thus far and coalescing it into a compelling personal vision statement. It's about defining your calling. Doing so brings you one step closer to truly experiencing the Inside-Out Effect and, therefore, closer to greater happiness, fulfillment, and effectiveness in both your professional and personal lives.

GOTTA HAVE VISION

As we said when we first introduced KNOW-BE-LEAD, whether we recognize it or not, *we are the leaders of our own lives.* We are the ones who determine our direction and who set our course through life. We are our own captains, our own CEOs. As the leaders of ourselves, it's crucial that we own the course we take through life. As the legendary GE CEO Jack Welch stated, great leaders ". . . create a vision, articulate the vision, passionately own the vision, and relentlessly drive it to completion."[1] Great leaders have *clear* and *compelling* visions. They motivate themselves and those around them by creating a vibrant, palpable North Star around which everyone's actions are motivated. Though we don't always think of ourselves as leaders, it's really quite easy to see how the vision we set for ourselves connects to the decisions we make and the actions we take. Over time, these life choices are directly related to how fulfilled we feel and how well we perform. The problem for those of us who are struggling from either a fulfillment or performance standpoint is that our current vision is not in alignment with our core self. We are not *compelled* by our vision. Simply put, the vision we've led our lives by is not our calling. Because of this, we've lost energy and focus. We've lost motivation and a sense of purpose in what we do. Perhaps our relationships, physique, and general health are failing. Today, we begin to change that. It's time to redefine and, perhaps for the very first time, write down our personal vision. Please grab a pen and some scratch paper. Get ready to mark up the next few pages.

CORE VALUES

At first glance, writing down your calling as a personal vision statement may feel like a pretty daunting task. In order to make it more manageable, we're going to begin with some lead-in questions that will help you synthesize the work you've done over the last couple of chapters and begin to distill your core values. You see, we look at core values as calling building blocks. They are the foundation upon which our callings are built. By flushing out your core values, you'll be able to converge upon the essential elements of your calling without having to immediately write it out as a vision statement. It's a nice and more importantly, useful, intermediate step.

To be clear, the values we're talking about when we say "core values" are those enduring ideas that fuel our personal fires, not those that motivate short-term, often ego-driven personal gains. Though the ego in us certainly values that next promotion or the acquisition of the next "it" thing (just ask Nate), those are not the values we're talking about here. Our core values have an intrinsic quality that transcends any external state or fleeting desire. Imbedded in the depths of our aware selves, they are our guiding lights—providing us with a meaningful barometer as we go through life.

All the work you've done thus far has put you in a great position to begin to hone in on your core values and formulate your calling. Don't worry about answering each of the following questions perfectly—remember, truly discovering and living your calling is

> "At the center of your being you have the answer; you know who you are and what you want."
>
> –Lao Tzu

an iterative process so you'll be able to continuously revisit this section in the days and months ahead. Just try to answer them with the same honesty and self-awareness you brought to the techniques we've presented thus far. Take a moment to gather your notes and thoughts from the first two KNOW chapters. Connect with them. Re-read them. Grab the SEE model you've been filling out. When you're good to go, generate thoughtful answers to each of the following questions and statements. Use them to help you hone in on your core values and calling.

1. **Describe moments where you truly come alive.**

_____

_____

_____

_____

2. **What's meaningful about these "alive" moments?**

_____

_____

_____

_____

_____

3. On your best day, how do you show up? (What version of you do you present to your colleagues? To your family? To your friends?)

_____

_____

_____

_____

_____

4. Who are the two people you respect and admire most? Describe what you admire about them.

_____

_____

_____

_____

_____

5. If, at the end of your life, you had lived the way you most wanted, how would others describe you?

_____

_____

_____

_____

_____

6. What would be inscribed on your tombstone?

_____

_____

_____

As we said, these six questions are meant to help you start co-alescing all of the work you've done so far and begin to zero-in on your core values. They are meant to help you begin to put the core parts of you—the parts that surround, influence, and define your calling—down on paper. Look back over your answers. Spend some time trying to glean your core values (perhaps they've come a long way from the exercise on page iii of the book). As you do so, feel free to write some of your core values on the lines below.

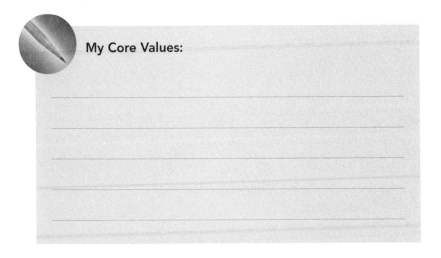

My Core Values:

_____

_____

_____

_____

_____

CALLING-VISION STATEMENT

At this point, you have a bevy of self-exploration insight, a well-used SEE model, and a list of core values. You've done powerful, important work, and now it's time to bring it all together. It's time to breathe life into your values and core perspectives by putting these things into an actionable construct: your Calling-Vision Statement (C-V Statement). You see, *knowing* your calling or *having* core values is not enough. They must be *lived*. As Jim Loehr and Tony Schwartz say in their book *Power of Full Engagement*, we must *live* our values so that they become virtues. They explain, "We may hold generosity as a value, but the virtue is *behaving* generously. Alignment occurs when we transform our values into virtues . . . For example: 'I demonstrate the value of generosity by investing energy in others, without expectation that I will receive anything in return, and by my willingness to put the agendas of those I care about ahead of my own, even if it means inconveniencing myself at times.'"[2] This is the purpose of your C-V Statement. It should serve as a guide for the *actions* you take. It is a map for how you will show up in every one of your interactions. Your C-V Statement illuminates the path to personal alignment, to living inside-out.

As you prepare to write a draft of your C-V Statement, we want to give you a few things to keep in mind as well as show you a few examples. The important things to remember when crafting your vision statement are summed up by what we call the **C3PO Rule** (those of you who are *Star Wars* fans should have a really easy time remembering this one). The C3PO Rule is that your C-V Statement should be:

1. *Clear.* It should be specific and articulate. Strive to make it easily understood, directive, and action oriented. Create a clean map for yourself.

2. *Compelling.* This is a big one. Does your C-V Statement inspire and move you? It must be motivational and far-reaching enough to pull you through difficult and uncertain times. We often say, "Extraordinary people have extraordinary visions." You are extraordinary. Prove it by making your vision compelling. (It's worth noting that this clear-compelling combination

has huge implications for behavior change and will be explored in depth in BE.)

3. _Concise._ While there is no precise length limit, your C-V Statement should be written in as few words as you think are needed. If it gets over a paragraph or two, you should probably be more concise.

4. _Present Tense._ This is a subtle but important point. Writing your C-V Statement in the present tense gives it power and immediately holds you to the standard you set for yourself. Cut out all "I will . . ." or "One day . . ." language. Beginning to try to live your calling starts now. Write it that way. Write "I am . . ."

5. _Others._ Your C-V Statement always has implications beyond yourself. When you change your behavior, you automatically start affecting and leading others differently. Be cognizant of that fact and make thoughtful considerations of how you can better affect others as part of your vision. Including others is more powerful and, in the long run, more rewarding.

Now that you have the C3PO Rule down, we want to share our C-V Statements with you as examples (you can also turn to _Nate's Status Update_ at the end of this chapter for another example). Here they are:

About the Authors: C-V Statements

Behnam's C-V Statement

I strive for the purpose of unconditional love and infinite, abundant energy, with powerful and inspirational presence to transform people, organizations, and countries while upholding my highest integrity.

My C-V Statement emerged like light in the darkness. It was the year 2000 and I was in the middle of a career breakdown (the same one I alluded to earlier when talking about my story). I was convinced that my best years were behind me and that it was all a gradual slope downwards from there. My relationships were suffering and my professional life had plateaued. After a seemingly endless number of months, I grew weary of the hopeless face staring back at me in the mirror every morning and decided to change something. After embarking on my own deep personal transformation journey, I came up with this C-V Statement, and it has changed everything. It enabled me to shift my focus from looking longingly over my shoulder to looking confidently at the path right in front of me. It opened me up to the abundant possibility of the present moment. I decided that I wanted to transform one hundred million people before I die! As a result of this vision, my last twelve years have been extraordinarily aligned and more fulfilling than I ever thought possible. They've also been incredibly productive. I've been able to publish five books on transformation, work with some of the leading organizations around the world, and have even gotten to advise the President of the United States. More than anything, I've been able to continuously pursue things that I love. This C-V Statement has been the fuel that ignites my life.

Michael's C-V Statement

My passion is empowering others to be more effective leaders, loving partners, and fulfilled people through authentic connection. As I help others catalyze change in their lives, I never lose sight of their ability to help me learn and evolve as well. I am committed to realizing dreams—for both myself and those I encounter. Above all else, I strive to lead a life of thoughtfulness, love, and happiness.

My C-V Statement came to fruition back when I was finishing up college. As I was preparing to graduate, I was mired with indecision about where to go next. I felt like a ship without a rudder. One night as I contemplated the next phase of my life, I spent a long time in quiet reflection. I remember closing my eyes, breathing, and trying to open myself up to the possibilities of the world. I sidestepped my fears and tried to put away any subconscious pressure I was putting on myself to pursue the "it" thing. After several hours, I was able to scribble down a rough draft of what would eventually become my C-V Statement. It has been a passion-filled guide for me ever since.

All the work you've done up to this point, through both the self-exploration techniques and the values identification exercise you just completed, has put you in a great position to take an initial crack at writing out your C-V Statement. We've eased into it, taking many of the necessary steps of self-discovery and reflection. Now it's time for you to give it a shot. As we've said all along, no part of this process is set in stone. The C-V Statement that you write down right now is not immutable—there can be plenty of refining down the road. However, you're now in the position to give it a very strong first go. Please, take the next 30 minutes to begin constructing your C-V Statement. Scribble a few iterations down on the scratch paper we asked you to grab earlier. When you feel like you have your best attempt at a first draft, please write it on the lines below. You will need to be able to reference it in the next chapter and throughout the rest of the book.

My Calling-Vision Statement:

_____

_____

_____

Your Calling Can Evolve: Lessons from Mother Teresa

An amazing example of the power of heeding your calling and being open to it changing over time can be found in Mother Teresa. Originally known as Agnes Gonxha Bojaxhiu, Mother Teresa was born into a relatively wealthy family in present-day Macedonia. From an early age, her parents instilled values of humility and charity, regularly taking in poor relatives and strangers alike. Her dad once told her, "Never eat a single mouthful unless you are sharing it with others."[3]

When Mother Teresa was nine, her father died. His passing devastated her family and changed her life profoundly. Though her family had always been quite religious, his death drew them even closer to the Catholic Church and compelled her to begin contemplating the religious life. At the age of 18, she felt a strong internal pull toward a religious life of service and she left home to join the Loreto Sisters, an Irish-based order of nuns that had missions in India. She would never see her family and friends again.

Mother Teresa embarked on her calling. Once she got to India, she spent her first few years teaching at a Catholic school, where the students were mainly girls from wealthy British and Indian families. Living in a relatively comfortable convent, she lived simplistically and immersed herself in theology. By age 27, she took her vows to become a nun and soon became both the principal of the Catholic school and the superior of the nuns at her convent—thus receiving the title of "Mother Teresa." However, after Mother Teresa had been in her position for nearly a decade, her predecessor returned to the school and convent to replace her. This devastated Mother Teresa and pushed her into a serious state of depression. As an Enneagram Two (Helper), this isn't too surprising, as Twos want and need to be appreciated for the work and care that they give. Mother Teresa's life now had a large void. She needed to figure out another way to help others and find personal meaning.

In an effort to help alleviate her depression, one of the Fathers she knew suggested she take a religious retreat to Darjeeling. During her train ride, she experienced what she referred to as her "call within a call" giving her the following message: "I was to leave the convent and help the poor while living among them. It was an order. To fail it would have been to break the faith."[4] This marked Mother Teresa's second calling iteration and, though she didn't know it then, would be the change that would take her from being a typical nun to becoming an amazing worldwide symbol of compassion and love.

Though initially it was difficult, she was patient and focused in her pursuit of her newfound calling. Because she was a nun, she had to wait for permission from the Loreto order in Ireland and the Catholic Church in Rome to leave the cloistered life as a nun and live among the people. After about a year, this permission was granted. She left the safe, comfortable living conditions of her Loreto convent and joined India's poor in the slums of Calcutta.

Setting out on her new life, she started by taking in and teaching kids from around the streets. Without a classroom of any sort and sitting in an open space among the poor's huts, she scrawled her lessons in the mud with a stick. After a year of demonstrating the viability of her situation, she was given papers from Rome allowing her to start her own order, the Missionaries of Charity, which helped her build out her following. Soon thereafter, she had the idea to create a place to house the dying. As the story goes, she came across a barely conscious woman on the pavement, half devoured by rats and wild dogs. Mother Teresa took the woman to the hospital but they were denied admission because the woman was too poor. It was then that she knew she had to do something. For the rest of her life, Mother Teresa committed herself to taking care of society's poorest and sickest. It was one of the most intrinsically meaningful things she could imagine. She professed, "A beautiful death is for people who lived like animals to die like angels—loved and wanted."[5] Her love manifested itself in her opening up these centers for the dying, dispensaries for the sick, and orphanages for abandoned and unwanted children in India and, eventually, throughout the world. She found her purpose in loving the unloved and wanting the unwanted.

For Mother Teresa, what started as her initial calling grew into another calling, which then grew into an idea, and then into an order, and ultimately, into an inspirational model for humanity to follow. Over the course of several versions of her calling vision, Mother Teresa built the strength and clarity in her life that led her to be the woman for which the world remembers her.

THE TOOLS
A SUMMARY

- Bringing together all of the work you've done from previous chapters, you are now ready to write down your C-V Statement.

- A highly helpful intermediate step is identifying your core values. Feel free to use our core value reflection questions to help with this process.

- Simply *having* core values or *having* a calling is useless. You must *live* your calling. Your C-V Statement sets the stage for you to do that.

- When you're ready to write down your C-V Statement, remember the **C3PO Rule:**
  - ◆ Clear
  - ◆ Compelling
  - ◆ Concise
  - ◆ Present Tense
  - ◆ Others

NATE'S STATUS UPDATE

After experiencing noticeable positive changes after just three weeks of heightening his self-awareness with the Enneagram, gratitude journal, PQ Reps, and authentic feedback process, Nate decided to stick with us through the whole KNOW-BE-LEAD framework. After all, he thought, if he could sense a little change just by learning more about himself and expressing some daily gratitude, he stood to experience significant change by committing to the entire transformation process.

Nate began the process of reaching his C-V Statement by gathering the work he had done over the course of KNOW thus far and answering our core value reflections questions. Here are his answers to several of them:

Q: Describe moments that give you the greatest sense of meaning.

A: *Life often feels most meaningful to me when I make new breakthroughs. Whether I'm in a professional or personal scenario, reaching a new conclusion or realization about a problem or obstacle is often very fulfilling for me. Also, interactions and relationships that are based on clear communication, mutual understanding, and authenticity give me a real sense of satisfaction and clarity. More than anything else, I derive meaning when I feel like I'm being a good father, an engaged and loving husband, and a progressive analyst and team leader for my firm.*

Q: Who are you at your best?

A: *At my best, I am full of energy and excitement. I am insightful, effective, and creative. I see situations not only for what they are but also for what they could be. I am a so-lution seeker rather than a problem perpetuator. Despite my confidence in my own opinion, I am patient and kind to others. I am committed to helping those who are important to me.*

Q: If, at the end of your life, you had lived the way you most wanted, how would others describe you? What would be inscribed on your tombstone?

A: *I hope others would describe me as someone who made things easier for them. They would hopefully see me as a truth-seeker and as someone who really cared. They would describe me as a man with a big imagination who channeled his creativity in meaningful and actionable ways. Others would say, despite my intellectual and professional interests, I always put the true loves of my life—my wife, children, and close friends—first. My tombstone would read something like this: "A man who loved exploring the BIG questions hand-in-hand with his beloved wife and beautiful children."*

When he was done, we asked him to review his answers and attempt to distill several of his most important core values. Here's what he came up with:

My Core Values:

Authenticity, health, intelligence, family, creativity, and communication.

As Nate prepared to write down his C-V Statement, he looked back over everything he had done so far—his Enneagram results, the nearly twenty-five entries he'd made in his gratitude journal, the letters he'd received through his peer feedback process, the sense of self he'd cultivated through PQ Reps, his answers to the reflection questions, and his core values. He then, at his own thoughtful pace, generated the following C-V Statement:

My ability to be the best I can be for others—whether it's my family, colleagues, friends, or new people I encounter— hinges on my ability to do best by myself. That means I make time for the things that mean the most to me on a regular basis. I make exercise and healthy habits a priority, even if they appear inconvenient. I spend time with my children and strive to create irreplaceable memories with them because I know that every moment with them is precious. I communicate openly, honestly, and most importantly, from a place of love with Chloe; I outwardly appreciate her everyday.

In my professional life, I am committed to doing work that invigorates me. I take on challenging projects that require creative solutions. I cultivate my own intellect as well as the intellects of my teammates energetically but patiently. I communicate authentically with both my colleagues and myself consistently—catching discontent and catalyzing change whenever necessary.

For Nate, this vision passed the C3PO Rule with flying colors. It was clear and directive. It was incredibly compelling. Though it wasn't short, he didn't feel like it was too verbose. It was in present tense and spoke directly to his impact and leadership with others. After writing it down and reading through it several times, Nate was incredibly excited for the new, more aligned direction he wanted to take his life. He was excited to start making changes.

LEAD

BE

KNOW

STEP TWO

BE: WHO
AM I BEING?

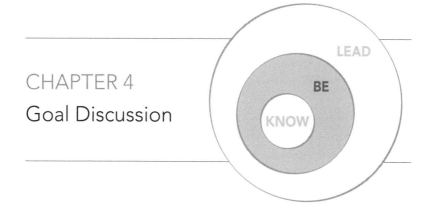

CHAPTER 4
Goal Discussion

To truly change ourselves, to succeed in forming new habits and patterns of behavior, we must first identify the targets for change—that is, the specific behaviors, routines, and attitudes we want to work on. The way we do that is by juxtaposing our current situation with the C-V Statement we've just written. To successfully do so requires honesty, courage, and—as we've cultivated throughout the KNOW part of our framework—self-awareness. It is time to progress to the next stage of KNOW-BE-LEAD. It's time to BE.

When many of the people we work with approach BE, they often say something along the lines of: "I've never really had a vision statement to act off of before." This means that their driving vision has basically been: "Take whatever comes along and make the best decisions I can." And this nondescript vision plagues many of us. Now, this isn't to say that we don't have a general direction. Most of us made a choice in our early adult years about the career track we wanted to pursue. We went into business, chose law, or became engineers, mechanics, or nurses. So let's not completely discredit ourselves; we did, at one point, choose a direction. However, since that choice, many of us have been on autopilot. We've pursued goals that come into our line of sight,

> All our dreams can come true—if we have the courage to pursue them."
> –*Walt Disney*

that are expected given the profession we've chosen. Up until now, many of us have been "roll with the punches" visionaries who have seldom asked ourselves the hard questions about our life's direction. We've settled with a vague, whimsical, and often highly misaligned and unfulfilling vision. Fortunately, we have now created and written down a C-V Statement built upon lengthy introspection and our core values. It's time for us to take an honest look at the reality of our current landscape, ask ourselves some hard questions, and, when all is said and done, identify our targets for change.

IS THIS MY DREAM?

Much like Nate, many of the people we work with come to us with the *is this it?* question. As we mentioned at the very beginning, they look at their job, their relationships, and their life in general and can't help but feel like something's missing. As we begin working with people on identifying change goals, we stress how important it is to honestly examine their current reality. They've completed their first foray through the self-discovery process, they've drafted their C-V Statement, and now they must have the courage to look at the current state of their life and ask, "Is this my calling? Is it my dream?" They have to ask, "Am I fulfilled by the life I'm living?"

Let us be the first to acknowledge that this direct line of self-questioning can be extremely hard to do. It's difficult because most of us, particularly those of us who really feel that underlying lack of satisfaction and fulfillment with our current circumstance, are afraid of the answers. We're afraid because answering means admitting to ourselves that we've made mistakes, we've wasted precious time, or we've in some way been missing *it*. And asking ourselves these cut-to-the-core questions means that we have to *provide* the answers; we have to provide *honest* answers. No more deluding ourselves with the wishy-washy "My job's alright" or "Even though my doctor-dad hounded me about med school since I was in middle school, being a physician is my dream . . . I think" responses. We've got to step up and level with ourselves. But doing so can be terrifying. It can be paralyzing. For many of us, passively settling for our current life or professional circumstance by labeling it "the way things are" is much easier than actively finding ways to improve our situation (remember, this doesn't mean you have to quit or change careers). Put simply, openly admitting to ourselves that we are dissatisfied with the current state of our work or life means admitting that we have inner turmoil. It means admitting that we haven't made the choices we wanted to make. It means pinpointing and exposing the sources of our unhappiness. This admission can bring on a large wave of cognitive dissonance,[1] a condition that the human mind constantly tries to resolve via self-delusion and internal storytelling—we all want to reduce the friction in our own minds. Thus, being able to successfully ask yourself these tough questions about your current circumstance requires heaps of courage. It requires a brave confidence that allows you to face your honest thoughts and expose the roots of your dissatisfaction. With courage, you can candidly admit the sources of your unfulfillment and poor performance without being dissuaded by fear and hopelessness. For us and the people we work with, this courage is fueled by a fundamental belief that *change is possible*. It's fueled by the knowledge that, by honestly answering the hard questions about our current situation, we can create well-formulated transformation goals that then comprise the foundation for an effective, well-targeted change plan.

CHASING THE WRONG DREAM[2]

Randy Komisar, a well-known Silicon Valley venture capitalist and the former CEO of LucasArts, is a great example of a man who forced himself to question the life he was building. He asked himself the hard questions and had the courage to search out the answers.

In the mid-1990s, Randy came to an inflection point in his career. He had just finished stints as CEO of LucasArts and subsequently as CEO of its rival, Crystal Dynamics, and was feeling incredibly rundown and unfulfilled by the work he had been doing. In an effort to change his life's trajectory, he began a regular meditation practice and courageously started questioning whether the life he had been living was really his dream. After a period of reflection, he realized that he had not been living in alignment with his values and his dream. Instead, he had been living in alignment with his father's.

Randy's dad was a fiercely competitive contract salesman. He valued material wealth above just about everything else and gambled constantly. From an early age, Randy learned from his father. He learned that success was totally predicated on the amount of money you earned and the status you could attain. As Randy says, "Insecurity about money was built into me as a child."

Over the course of his reflection, Randy realized that he needed to let go of the dream he had adopted from his father. He needed to revaluate his goals and aspirations. He says:

I was on the fast track, but it wasn't my track. There was a war inside me between the need to be fulfilled versus the desire to be successful in my father's eyes and of society. It was time to let go of the notion I was climbing the ladder of success and accept the fact that I was on a long and winding journey.

As Randy came to this conclusion, he was able to let go of his dad-instilled vision and re-chart his course.

> " Be yourself; everyone else is already taken."
> –Oscar Wilde

He was able to grow in self-awareness and start pursuing a life more in line with his core self and core values. He eventually became a venture capitalist and now spends his time helping leaders in companies that he finds meaningful. He helps them grow their businesses and, equally as important, helps them grow themselves.

GOALS

When we begin to juxtapose our C-V Statement with the realities of our current circumstance, we immediately begin finding targets for change and growth; we begin finding goals. This transition to goal-setting marks a significant inflection point in our framework. It marks the transition from calling exploration and identification to actual change planning. It is the transition from self-discovery to self-commitment, from KNOWING to BEING.

Determining our transformation goals is the first step in the change implementation process. As such, it is the first formal juncture where people ask themselves: "In what ways do I actually want to change my life?" This question, coupled with all of the work we've done so far, sometimes leaves people wide-eyed and thinking things like: "Since I'm not fulfilled and underperforming at work, do I have to quit my job?" "I realize my calling is something else entirely. Do I have to drop everything and change?" or "My husband doesn't bring me the sense of happiness that he used to, is it over?" These are big questions and, in light of all the self-discovery we've embarked on thus far, are relevant ones for many of you. However, we want to reassure you that we fundamentally believe that every single person can make huge strides toward their calling without having to turn their life upside down. We believe that there exist more optimal, fulfilling, and rewarding paths in your current situation and environment. If you so choose, we are committed to helping you find and live them. So please, dispel any notions that you'll have to pack a suitcase and move to Tanzania to do relief work for the rest of your life, or that you have to divorce your spouse and move to an ashram. Living in greater alignment with your calling often starts by pursuing manageable, incremental goals we like to call **Tweak Goals**.

That said, some of you will end up thinking—despite the potential progress that could be made in your current career, with your current organization, or in your current relationship— that it won't be enough. You'll feel (or perhaps already do) that drastic change is a precursor to beginning to experience your life as a calling, that a monumental switch is a requirement for re-discovering the purpose and performance in your life. You might feel that you need to change careers. You're certain that going to a different company would do wonders. Or you're confident about the need to either leave or make significant changes to your relationship. We call these big ticket, smack-you-in-the-gut goals **Overhaul Goals.** If you go through the goal identification process and after enough calm and thoughtful time find yourself realiz-ing that you have Overhaul Goals, you're probably right. While you'll make strides with Tweak Goals, your discontent is great enough to where you need a change of scenery. It may not be that you need to move to the other side of the world, but you may feel like you need to make drastically different choices. Though these types of goals are more daunting, trust yourself if you feel confidently that Tweak Goals won't be enough. You're at a place of heightened self-awareness; have the courage to listen to what will most fulfill you.

Regardless of what your goal landscape ends up looking like, the goal-setting process can be difficult. As the transition between realization and preparing for action, goal identification is often a time where people are caught between knowing what they should do and hesitating about what they "in reality" can do. People often put significant pressure on themselves and can sometimes become overwhelmed by both the implications and work presented by certain goals. Therefore, before we dive into the actual goal-setting process, we want to spend some time addressing the common concerns people have when formulating their goal list. We'll do so by goal type.

ANTICIPATING TENSION: TWEAK GOALS

Concern #1: My goal isn't drastic enough.

Perhaps the biggest concern people have with Tweak Goals is that they aren't significant enough. People look at their Tweak Goals and see too much of the status quo and too little hard-hitting change. Our response and our advice to you if you find yourself thinking something along these lines when you're coming up with your goals is to not underestimate the power of the small changes.

For example, consider the profound role of perspective. Since we were young, most of us have heard adages about the power of our attitude. We've heard things along the lines of "attitude affects outcome," "the power of positive thinking," and "believe in yourself." Despite our learned eye roll response to have-a-good-attitude pep talks, we (the authors) are ardent believers. We know that there is tremendous power in your fundamental view.

Jorge, a debt collector for Santa Clara County and one of our clients, is a great example of this. On the very first day we started working with him and his team, we talked with him about the

The secret to having it all is knowing you already do."

–Unknown

impact a compelling fundamental view of his work could have on him. Almost despairingly, he admitted, "Honestly, I have a miserable job. I spend the majority of my time each day trying to collect loan payments from this county's impoverished people, people who have almost nothing as it is. I can't see what's compelling about that." Though we empathized with Jorge's position, we asked him to consider another fundamental view. What if, we proposed, instead of looking at his job as being a cruel collector, he saw himself as a conscientious distributor? After all, the county has limited resources and the money he was trying to collect was money his department wanted to lend to other people in need. It was going to people who hadn't yet had the benefit of a loan or other financial services. We reminded him that he could simultaneously work to collect payments and redistribute aid while still being kind to those he was trying to collect from. In fact, between those two sides of his situation resided his opportunity to be a creative solution seeker—a person who compassionately worked with poor people on behalf of other poor people. After letting our words marinade for about a minute, Jorge broke into a smile. "Yeah, I guess I could give that a shot," he said. Over the rest of the time we worked with him, not only did Jorge become one of the most upbeat members of his team, he also became one of the most passionate. It's amazing what a little tweak in perspective can do.

The importance and impact of one's perspective has also been showcased via research. Through various studies, Yale psychologist Amy Wrzesniewski has found that "satisfaction with life and with work may be more dependent on how an employee sees his or her work than on income or occupational prestige."[3] In a study with her colleague Jane Dutton, Wrzesniewski reinforced the power of perspective by comparing two groups of hospital cleaners. One group of cleaners said that they experienced their work mundanely. They saw it simply as a job—a tedious, repetitive series of tasks. The other group saw themselves as important caretakers of the hospital. They interacted with patients more, and approached their work with a noticeably higher energy level then their counterparts. Not surprisingly, because the cleaners in the second group perceived their work as meaningful (and subsequently acted accordingly), they were happier and more satisfied with the work they did. Dutton and Wrzesniewski have found the same trend across a large swath of industries and countless numbers of workers. A subtle change in perspective can go a long way.

The moral of the story is don't underestimate the power of the small changes. If over the course of your goal-setting process, you encounter the "is this drastic enough?" concern, think about how impactful something as simple as reorienting your perspective toward your work can be. May it reassure you that simple changes, no matter how small, can often be quite profound.

Concern #2: My goal is so subtle. Are these subtleties really feasible?

Another big concern for people looking at a list of Tweak Goals revolves around feasibility. Because Tweaks aren't Overhauls, it's usually not the overwhelming "my God, how can I ever get the gumption to do this?" feasibility concern. Rather, because Tweaks involve intentional changes in situations that you're already so familiar with, in situations where your behavior has already been significantly conditioned, it's more of the "how will I ever recondition myself to act and see things differently in such familiar waters?" feasibility concern. With Tweak Goals, you're sticking with the same company, relationship, and similar routine to what you had before rather than making sweeping changes like a career switch or a large geographical move. In the midst of so much familiarity, you must be extra vigilant about pursuing your goals. For those who have these feasibility concerns, think about the following two tidbits.

First, just because you aren't changing companies, relocating, or switching careers, doesn't mean you can't fight to create perceptible change for yourself. Put yourself out there in ways you don't normally. Take your current scenario, whatever it may be, and live at risk. Or, as we like to say, live at **RISC** (see Figure 13). Approach your work with a sense of **R**esponsibility. Though we don't always think about it, our work *matters*. It's on us to do it and do it well. Hold yourself and others to a high standard and the meaning in what you do will increase. Step up your **I**nvolvement in new projects and initiatives. Plan the next company event. Volunteer to help on a new product brainstorm. Propose something new for your team. As you do, the way you see and experience your organization will evolve— remember, as you get out of your comfort zone, good things happen. If you feel like things have really stagnated, try to **S**witch teams or departments. A fresh group of people could go a long way toward helping you become reinvigorated. Finally, **C**hallenge yourself. Being in the same place for a long time is enough to sap the zest out of even the most energetic people. Push yourself even when your boss or your colleagues aren't. Learn a new skill set. Go above and beyond on a project for your own growth and creativity. In so doing, you will develop yourself as an employee, as a person, and as someone who finds what they do meaningful. Remember, you're in familiar waters but subtle changes can be significant. You are not bound to the same routine.

RESPONSIBILITY

INVOLVEMENT

SWITCH

CHALLENGE

FIGURE 13

What are some potential ways you can live more at RISC at your current job through a Tweak Goal?

Responsibility: _____

_____

Involvement: _____

_____

Switch: _____

_____

Challenge: _____

_____

> When we are children, we live in a world of limited capabilities but boundless possibility. Sadly, as we age, we limit our possibilities in the face of boundless capability. We must forget what it means to be 'grown up.'"
>
> –Behnam Tabrizi

Another way to alleviate your concern about whether your Tweak Goals are feasible is by searching out "positive outliers."[4] "Positive outliers" are moments in the past where something has gone well, moments where you have felt a sense of meaning and purpose in your career and life in general. (We'll delve more into this in our section on goal formation.) For whatever goal you're considering, search out these moments in your memory. If your goal is to be a more empathetic leader, scour your memory for a moment where you felt like you really listened and related to one of your team members. What types of things did you do? How did you know you had connected? Try to remember the little details if you can—not only will remembering alleviate the concern you have about whether or not your subtle Tweak Goal is possible, but it will also give you insight into how to go about pursuing the goal and changing your behavior. The lessons of past successes are hidden gems. Seize them and try to grasp their subtleties. They will give you reassurance and confidence as you decide which Tweak Goals you most want to pursue.

All in all, just because Tweak Goals don't appear as big and drastic as Overhaul Goals on paper, it doesn't mean that they're easy (though they sometimes can be, which is great!). For those of you who experience some of this struggle, please re-reference this section for help in overcoming your concerns and gaining confidence in your ability to succeed. As you do, you'll find that despite not making an overhaul change to your current situation, career, or relationship, you'll begin growing closer to your calling.

ANTICIPATING TENSION: OVERHAUL GOALS

Concern #1: Is it too late?

In the realm of Overhaul Goals, people are usually concerned if not downright threatened by the magnitude of the proposed change. Even though they know they could, on some level, improve their sense of fulfillment and performance using more digestible Tweak Goals, they know it won't be enough. For these people to truly live their calling, they know that they have to make a drastic change. But even though they can feel it within them, there is still tension; there is still fear. One of the biggest concerns that rises to the forefront of their minds is: "Is it too late?"

Dr. Ken Robinson, the author of *The Element: How Finding Your Passion Changes Everything*, devotes an entire chapter to answering this question. In it, he shares over fifteen stories of people who found and began living their calling (or, as he calls it, their "element") in the later decades of their lives. He shares the story of the best-selling author Harriet Doerr who, after raising a family, returned to the realm of formal education at the age of sixty-five. She ended up studying in Stanford's creative writing program, and eight years later published *Stones for Ibarra*, her National Book Award–winning first book. He describes how Julia Child spent the first part of her professional life working in advertising and in several U.S. government jobs. It wasn't until her mid-thirties that she took an interest in French food and began taking professional culinary courses. Nearly a decade and a half later, she published *Mastering the Art of French Cooking*, and she began her rise to the forefront of the American home cooking and TV cooking show world. The world famous Russian-American pianist Vladimir

Horowitz performed his last recital tour at the age of eighty-four. When she was eighty, Jessica Tandy won the Best Actress Oscar. Benjamin Franklin invented bifocals at the age of seventy-eight. And the stories go on and on.

Robinson does acknowledge that, particularly when it comes to physical feats, there are some limitations on when it actually becomes "too late." If you want to win an Olympic gold medal, triumph in the Mr. Universe bodybuilding competition, or play in the NBA, there are certainly ages where it's safe to say that you're probably "too late." However, for the vast majority of pursuits, chronological age is fairly unimportant. Whether you're discovering and pursuing your calling at twenty-eight or eighty-two, all that matters is the energy, creativity, and desire you have behind your goals. So many times, the people who are at the age or point in their lives where they wonder "is it too late?" are only focused on all the experiences that have taught them to be wary, to be suspicious of change and risk adverse. While some of those thoughts are healthy and certainly have moments where they help them on their path, there are countless other experiences that have put them in an even better position to go for it. Experience in the ways of the world, connections and friendships across a variety of industries and places, and a sense of wisdom that comes from living, loving, losing, and traveling are all benefits we enjoy as we age.

Society tries to convince us that life is a linear, one-way street that consist of birth–elementary school–middle school–high school diploma–college degree–45-year career (complete with 401k, medical benefits, and paid vacation)–house (complete with family, mortgage, and an SUV)–retirement–death. The reality is that life can have incredible twists and turns as long as we are open to new opportunities and willing to follow our core self when they present themselves and resonate with us. As Robinson wonderfully puts it at the end of his chapter:

[What people like Julia Child] teach us is that remarkable, life-enhancing things can happen when we take the time to step out of our routines, rethink our paths, and revisit the passions we left behind (or never pursued at all) for whatever reason. We can take ourselves in a fresh directions at nearly any point in our lives. . . . As the actor Sophia Loren once said, "There is a fountain of youth: it is your mind, your talents, the creativity you bring to your life and the lives of the people you love. When you learn to tap this source, you will truly have defeated age."[5]

Concern #2: What about the money?

The other, often gargantuan, concern that people facing Overhaul Goals have revolves around money. Namely, they fear that they won't be able to make "enough" money if they switch from their career to their calling. Let us start by saying that this, in most cases, is a very real concern. We live in a world where money makes things easier (at least up to certain quantities). If your lifestyle is or aspires to be anything like Nate's, for instance, you have a spouse, a mortgage, children, dental bills, groceries, retirement funds, and vacations to support and pay for. Swapping your human resources managerial position for a first-year teaching salary might not be a good financial move if you have dependents and a bunch of hefty recurring bills like Nate does. However, many of the people we work with who are beginning to consider career Overhaul Goals usually aren't weighing a trade-off between comfortable salary and struggle-to-pay-my-bills salary (if that's the trade-off, nearly everyone opts for improving their current work situation as best they can via Tweak Goals). No, those who are concerned about money issues and are still considering career Overhaul Goals usually have anxiety about transitioning from a very handsome salary to a more moderate but doable salary. For those of you in that situation, check out the following research.

Psychologist David Myers, author of *The Pursuit of Happiness* and several in-depth, cross-cultural studies about the relationship between material wealth and happiness, has found an extremely low correlation between conventional wealth and happiness. He describes, "We humans need food, rest, warmth and a social contract. . . . For starving Sudanese and homeless Iraqis money would buy more happiness. But having more than enough provides little additional boost to well-being."[6] Material wealth beyond what we require to take care of our basic needs, he says, barely registers as an indicator for greater happiness and meaning. In fact, he says that in the United States the correlation between them is zero. Not only does Myers say that money beyond what we need has virtually no direct impact on our sense of fulfillment and happiness, but he has also found it to be relatively independent of other well-being indicators. "Income also doesn't noticeably influence satisfaction with marriage, family, friendship or ourselves— all of which do predict a sense of well-being," he says.[7]

Myers' findings are consistent with the research we presented at the beginning of the book that showed how, around the world, well-being has suffered even as many countries (the United States included) have continued to grow wealthier. His findings also align with research done by Nobel Prize–winning economist Daniel Kahneman. He and his team found the following regarding the connection between wealth and satisfaction: "The belief that high income is associated with good mood is widespread but mostly illusory. People with above-average income are relatively satisfied with their lives but are barely happier than others in moment-to-moment experience, tend to be more tense, and do not spend more time in particularly enjoyable activities."[8]

So, as you can see, material wealth is in a nuanced position. It's certainly a contributor to our happiness and well-being (and therefore performance) to the point that it helps us take care of our basic needs, support our children, pay our bills, and cover the costs of running our households. However, beyond that point, it's relatively ineffective at generating greater meaning in our lives. Sure, it can facilitate satisfying life experiences like a family trip or a show downtown, but excess money can also cause stress and anxiety (think stock market volatility, money-leeching extended family). What's more is that the contemporary research we've just discussed shows that it's all relatively inconsequential. For those of you really weighing this concern, another thing to consider is that past decisions in the favor of money and material wealth are probably significant contributors to why you are here at this unfulfilled crossroads. For a lot of us, it's the reason we don't just pursue our calling in the first place! We leave school and have thoughts like *We'd love to pursue acting, but society, our parents, and ourselves insist that being a lawyer is a smarter financial choice. We think it could be cool to do social work with kids, but it won't give us the financial runway we desire. We think we could make a phenomenal schoolteacher, but corporate sales is where the money is.*

Try it out!

1. What is the calling career you're considering?

2. Estimate your long-term monthly income for this new career:

3. Try living by that budget for the next month. Can you do it?

It's okay to have qualms about how your salary might change as a result of changing your career. It's a difficult situation because you're comparing something that's inherently quantifiable (salary) to something that's intrinsically unquantifiable (your sense of fulfillment and meaning). However, in this situation don't mistake quantifiable for valuable and unquantifiable for less so. You're here right now because you've had a core realization that more is not always *more*. Trust the research. Trust us. And, above all else, trust yourself. If you know that making a career change is essential for your sense of purpose and happiness and that doing so leaves you in a comfortable and feasible financial situation, we encourage you to overcome your fear, act with courage, and make the choice that you've been denying yourself for so long. You can do it.

Overhauling Her Life[9]

After receiving her B.A. in Economics from UCLA, Leah Kim took a job working at a large financial firm as a wealth manager. At first, it seemed like she had taken the first step of a bright professional arc. She had landed a job that her friends all envied and that everyone said would put her on the path to success and happiness. It didn't take long for things to turn though, and after just a few months, as she was on the phone with a wealthy client, she realized that the happiness she felt when describing her life to people was not a feeling that propped her up when nobody was there asking her those questions. She wanted to spend her time helping people whose lives could be improved as a result of her actions. She wanted purpose.

Fearful of change but knowing that it was necessary, Leah made the conservative move to a smaller, more specialized financial firm in the hopes that she'd find happiness in a new environment. When she got there though, things were worse than ever. She was having the same conversations with the same kinds of people, and she felt less fulfilled than ever before. One Friday morning, she woke up and couldn't take it anymore. She knew deep within that she had to overhaul her life. She quit before lunch that same day.

With six months of savings to keep her afloat and no direction in sight, Leah started filling her empty days with yoga. She immediately connected with the physicality of it, the way it made her feel like her soul was stretching along with her muscles. She would volunteer, clean the mats, sweep the floors, or restock the bathrooms just to have more time at her local studio. She loved being in and helping create this magical place, both a location and a state of mind, where stress would yield to love and peace. She wanted to be there every day, in those poses.

Soon she had enrolled in and completed her instructor training classes. Within a few months, she began teaching yoga in LA. Her students loved her and the rosters grew. Before long, she was teaching 25 classes a week. The momentum was finally there, building with each pose of each day. She moved to Hong Kong and did the same thing, teaching classes constantly throughout the week, until she came to a point where her exhausted body couldn't keep up with her desire to share her passion. A friend suggested that she look for less intense project-based teaching engagements: high-end gyms, corporate work, and retreats. She gave it a shot.

Today, Leah is the Ambassador for Nike's Global Yoga Program. She teaches a small number of clients each day and spends much of her time in meditation. Yoga was the tool that allowed her to make the transition from a life based on satisfying external expectations to a life of internal peace. Now, she focuses on enriching her life to make her work life more interesting. Her favorite pose is the child's pose, kneeling on the floor in a bowing position, your face literally on the earth. She says that she's "wowed by the feeling" that she gets while in that pose, and loves being challenged with difficult poses that incorporate calmness, grace, and flow. Every time she moves into a pose, she feels her full presence in the moment, mindful and aware. When she speaks to clients or conferences about her story, she advises people to dream bigger, because "The things that will actually happen will be bigger than you can possibly dream up."

THE ROLE OF GOALS

As we prepare to embark on the goal-setting process, we want to make sure we're clear on how we see the role of goals. For us, change goals are the fundamental building blocks of the personal transformation process. They are the guiding lights that continually lead us into greater alignment with our calling. They spur us forward.

That said, the bulk of their value does not lie in their attainment. Our happiness, fulfillment, and most effective selves don't simply reside at the point where we reach our goals. Instead, they are nurtured and developed along the way. Setting goals is a freeing exercise. Once we select them and build them into our personal change plan, we are free to live in alignment in the only place we can—the current moment. Selecting goals in line with our calling, in line with our true selves and values, sets our ship in the right direction. They are a means to begin living in greater alignment with our calling, not just an ends. Let's now prepare to honestly examine our current landscape in light of our newly formed vision statement. In the next chapter we will take the first step toward change by forming our initial goals.

THE TOOLS
A SUMMARY

- To begin moving toward goal-setting, you must have the courage to honestly look at your current circumstance and juxtapose it with your C-V Statement.

- Doing so can be an anxiety filled process so we'd like to anticipate some tensions:
  - ◆ For Tweak Goals:
    - Is my goal drastic enough?
      - ○ Research and experience have shown that small changes can have a tremendous impact (i.e., change in attitude/perspective)
    - Is such a subtlety even feasible?
      - ○ Sure it is, begin to live at RISC (Responsibility, Involvement, Switch, Challenge)
      - ○ Search for positive outliers—past moments where, even for a glimmer, you experienced the positive thing you're seeking.
  - ◆ For Overhaul Goals:
    - Is it too late?
      - ○ No. It's really not.
    - What about the money?
      - ○ Extensive research by world-class psychologists and economists shows that income has very little direct impact on our fulfillment and happiness past the point that it covers our essential needs.

- Remember the role of goals: they are guiding lights that enable us to set out in the direction of alignment. They are means as well as ends. Fulfillment isn't just found in attaining them. It's found in every step along the path.

CHAPTER 5

Goal Formation

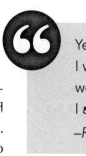

The juxtaposition of our current circumstance with our calling should provide a number of areas where we'd like to make changes. We encourage you to choose the two or three

> "Yesterday I was clever, so I wanted to change the world. Today I am wise, so I am changing myself."
> –Rumi

most obviously misaligned areas to begin formulating your initial transformation goals. As with our KNOW exercises, we strongly recommend that you write these goals down (we've included space at the end of the chapter). Interact with them; think through them. They don't have to be perfect and they don't have to be pretty. They just need to represent an initial commitment toward changing a behavior or attitude that doesn't fit with your calling. To help you identify these targets for change, please read through the following goal-identification techniques. Feel free to utilize any that resonate with you.

MIRACLE AND EXCEPTION QUESTIONS

As we alluded to in our discussion about Tweak Goals, "positive outliers" can be used to catalyze change. By using positive outliers, rather than focusing our change efforts on avoiding and fixing what's wrong, we can focus our efforts on recreating what's right. Instead of embodying the common mindset of "less of the bad," it frequently helps to channel our energy into the perspective: "How do we get more of the good?" This method can be extremely beneficial as we actually try to break our calling down into actionable goals in both our work and home lives.

Specifically, positive outliers are used explicitly in a couple of insightful methods from solutions-focused brief therapy (SFBT).[1] For quick context, SFBT is a style of therapy developed in the late 1970s that, unlike many traditional forms of therapy, does not particularly care about or dwell in someone's past. Instead, it's a type of therapy that is solely focused on fixing the problem at hand. Accordingly its techniques are direct and solutions-centric. There are two methods from SFBT that can help us to uncover our positive outliers and target areas for change. The methods are called the Miracle and Exception Questions.[2]

First, the Miracle Question. After describing your problem, irk, or troubles, a solutions-focused counselor will ask you something along the lines of: "If, while you slept tonight, some kind of miracle occurred that completely alleviated your pain or fixed your condition, what would be your first small sign upon waking that everything was better?" People often initially misinterpret the question and respond by describing how everything would be different—they describe the entire change miracle. However, this is not the question. The question is: What is the *first sign* that things had changed? What is that first small thing, that first interaction that would indicate that your problem had been solved? See the following example of Michael using the Miracle Question with Annabel, a mid-level manager at a medical device company trying to make her career more of a calling.

Michael: . . . And, upon walking into the office in the morning, what would be the first sign that you were no longer bored or disillusioned with work? What would be the first indicator that things were different?

Annabel: I don't know. I suppose I'd feel differently. My team would probably greet me differently too.

Michael: What does "differently" mean? For both your feelings and your team's greeting.

Annabel: For me, I guess it means that I'd be excited to be at work. I'd cross the threshold with high energy and a sense of focus. And for my team, they'd actually greet me for a change. They'd say "hello" and smile. There would be a sense of camaraderie and teamwork.

Michael: And what makes you excited at work?

Annabel: Hmm . . . I get excited, or at least hopeful, anytime I'm able to take a break from the daily grind and think about the people's lives that are touched and changed by our products. You know, picture their faces and their families. It makes me feel like I'm doing something that matters.

Though Michael doesn't come out and explicitly say *What's your goal for changing your attitude and performance at work?* he alludes to it through the Miracle Question. The Miracle Question allows Annabel to visualize her problem actually being fixed in a day-in-my-life scenario. She's able to imagine and visualize progress. And rather than asking her a top-down, *what's the goal?* question, this process enables her to develop specific, manageable change targets from the inside-out. Through just this brief line of questioning, Annabel has a great potential target for change:

Change Goal: Cross the threshold at work everyday with a sense of excitement and energy.

Potential Method: *Visualize the consumers your products help everyday.*

You can do the same. As you are trying to develop targets for change, sit down and ask yourself what your first sign would be that you were living more in line with your calling, more in line with your vision statement. What would you do as you wake up? How would you feel? How would you start the Monday morning meeting? Trace your gut responses until you get concrete answers. Ask yourself to define overly general or fuzzy words. What do they mean in terms of how you act?

Miracle Question: *Choose a particular area you're struggling with. If tomorrow you woke up and things in that area had miraculously gotten better, what would be **the first** sign indicating that that was the case?*

Area I'm Struggling With:_____

_____

First Sign Things Are Better:_____

_____

_____

As we'll dive into later, change is most successful when it is done in small, manageable chunks. The Miracle Question enables people to actually visualize the tip of the change iceberg in their mind's eye. It breaks change down into an initial feasible part—a perfect initial target or goal for change.

Now, the Exception Question. After a solution-focused counselor has helped someone visualize a manageable, detailed change goal through the Miracle Question, she then asks them something like: "When was the last time you experienced this miracle, this first hint of change, even if it was just for an instant?" You see, even though people often see their life, job, or circumstance as all one way, the reality is that there has been *an exception* at some point. Thus, a solutions-focused counselor not only helps her client imagine a positive outlier, she shows the client that the positive outlier has, at some point, actually occurred in their life. Where the Miracle Question enables someone to visualize and establish initial goals for change, the Exception Question provides hope that change is possible. It motivates. It says, "See, you've done this before." In a very sneaky way, it provides proof that people are capable of the change they desire because they, at least in certain moments, have already experienced the change. The positive outliers that people identify not only serve as hopeful examples, but also as mini case studies for discovering circumstances, attitudes, and actions that facilitate the change that people desire. Here's our use of the Exception Question with Annabel:

> **Michael:** When was the last time you were excited as you crossed the parking lot heading into work?
>
> **Annabel:** Well, during my first four years here, I was excited a lot. I felt like I was a part of something big, a part of a company that was helping people in a deep way. It was a vibe that was shared by a lot of my teammates back then too.
>
> **Michael:** How did you know that you were helping people so profoundly?
>
> **Annabel:** I don't know—it's the nature of our business. You know, med devices. Oh, and . . . wait . . . our customer service team used to share client testimonials and stories in a weekend newsletter every week. They were often topics of conversation in the break room on Mondays. Lots of people would talk about them, especially on the team I was on. I can't believe I didn't realize they're not doing that anymore. Now that

I'm managing more people, I haven't paid attention to all of the little things that don't pertain directly to my team as much.

Michael: *So you don't regularly share and discuss customer stories and testimonials with your team the way your manager did with you during your initial years at the company?*

Annabel: (Somewhat sheepishly) *No . . . no, I guess I don't.*

Though our exploration of the Exception Question leaves Annabel feeling a little guilty about something she's let go by the wayside, it was incredibly helpful because it allowed her to make some realizations about how to go about changing her and her team's attitude (and, accordingly, performance) at work. Bring back the customer stories. Post them on the walls and on the bathroom stalls. Make the people who use and benefit from her company's products come alive. Their stories are compelling, they're motivating, and, if she implements it well, they could be one of the keys to reinvigorating her workplace.

Just as with the Miracle Question, use the Exception Question as you begin identifying change targets. If part of your C-V Statement is to bring out the best in those you work with, when was the last time you acknowledged someone's performance at the office? Even if you struggle with it, when was the last time you truly empowered someone you manage? What can you learn from that instance to apply to this personal transformation effort?

Exception Question: *Given your answer to the Miracle Question in the previous section, when was the last time you experienced that **first sign**, if only for a moment?*

_____

_____

_____

By using these two questions, we promise you will be able to focus in on small, actionable starting points for change as well as discover motivation and reassurance that *change is possible*. Use these questions to identify your change goals and the potential methods therein. Soon, as we embark on implementing change, you will learn to seize and replicate the positive outliers in your life. In so doing, you will grow closer to your calling, peak performance, and happiness.

YOUR IDEAL DAY

Inspired by the first time we read Mitch Albom's *Tuesdays with Morrie*, this technique involves taking time—real time—to think about your ideal day. For quick context, *Tuesdays with Morrie* is the true story about a series of visits Mitch has with his 79-year-old former professor, Morrie, who is dying of Lou Gehrig's disease. As he moves closer to death, Morrie uses their visits as opportunities to dispense insightful wisdom and poignant advice about life, love, and what's truly important. Near the end of his professor's life, Mitch asks Morrie what his perfect day would consist of if he were suddenly healthy again. Having had many weeks to contemplate his life, to mull over the stuff that is truly important at his core, Morrie responds directly and simply. Faced with the end, he understands exactly who he is and what is important to him. Accordingly, he has an intuitive sense about what his perfect day would be like.

Though very few of us are in Morrie's exact situation, his example is inspirational. To know what's important to us and to be able to honestly examine our day-to-day life through that lens is immeasurably powerful. Fortunately, with all of the introspection and self-discovery you've done thus far, you have developed a very strong sense of your core self—perhaps a stronger sense than you've ever had before. To help flush out your change goals, jot down the answer to the following question: How, in light of your self-awareness, would your ideal day look? Think about the question in the context of work. Think about it in the time you spend with your children. What about on the weekends? Slightly more involved than the Miracle and Exception Questions, the Ideal Day exercise helps you put your calling into an actual day or week framework and therefore makes it more readily comparable to the way you currently spend your time.

After you get your ideal day(s) down on paper, see how it compares to your actual days. Note areas of significant difference. Which of these gaps are feasible starting points for change? Obviously, this technique is not about turning your day-to-day life into a pipe dream life. It's not about finding areas of your life to make more fantasy-like. It's about finding areas where you can begin to bring your current life into more alignment with your most meaningful life. On your best day, what do you do?

"Let's see . . . I'd get up in the morning, do my exercises, have a lovely breakfast of sweet rolls and tea, go for a swim, then have my friends come over for a nice lunch. I'd have them come one or two at a time so we could talk about their families, their issues, talk about how much we mean to each other. Then I'd go for a walk, in a garden with some trees, watch their colors, watch the birds, take in the nature that I haven't seen in so long now. In the evening, we'd all go together to a restaurant with some great pasta, maybe some duck—I love duck— and then we'd dance the rest of the night. I'd dance with all the wonderful dance partners out there, until I was exhausted. Then I'd go home and have a deep, wonderful sleep."

"That's it?"

"That's it."

144

It was so simple. So average. I was actually a little disap-
pointed. I figured he'd fly to Italy or have lunch with the Presi-
dent or romp on the seashore or try every exotic thing he
could think of. After all these months, lying there unable to
move a leg or a foot—how could he find perfection in such
an average day?

Then I realized this was the whole point.

—Morrie Schwartz and Mitch Albom, *Tuesdays with Morrie*[3]

REAL-TIME NOTES

Much of Behnam's early career as an academic and as a consultant revolved around the notion of real-time systems, enterprises, and organizations. By real-time we mean systems or processes without lag time. The benefits of such systems are widely documented, particularly in industry. Real-time organizations have better information flow, quicker decision making, and often more transparency. After working with a number of people on personal transformation, we've found the real-time notion to be extremely applicable to personal change goal-setting as well. Specifically, we've developed a technique we've dubbed Real-Time Notes.

Much like the Ideal Day technique, Real-Time Notes is a largely self-described technique. It involves keeping close tabs on yourself over the course of several days. Keep a notebook on your desk, use your phone to record notes, or keep a pad of Post-It notes in your back pocket—whatever works for you. Then, throughout the day, write down the moments that you feel out of alignment, unhappy, or dissatisfied as they happen. If you don't perform well, jot it down. If your team is struggling, write down the specific triggers and moments. If you come home to a grudge match with your spouse, note that and the circumstances surrounding it.

After a handful of days of keeping Real-Time Notes, look over all of your entries. Put them all next to your C-V Statement. Begin by comparing these strife-laden moments to your calling. How, in light of your core values and true self, would you have handled a given moment better? What might you have done differently? After you work through the list, try to assign some priority. Search out the entries that seem particularly discordant with your vision statement. What goals can you set around improving your behavior or attitude in these particularly misaligned instances? How can you improve and move closer to your calling?

The Real-Time Notes technique works because it creates a physical record of your current circumstances as they happen. It can sometimes be difficult to see the nuances of your current situation when you're simply reflecting back on past events. It's another thing entirely to see them precisely recorded on paper. (On that note, for those of you who used the journaling technique for self-discovery in KNOW, depending on how exactly you implemented it, it's possible that you might have some good starting material for Real-Time Notes.) Here's a one-day example of how we usually ask clients to record events with this method:

6:35 am: My husband is already out of bed. Probably reading the paper as the kids get ready for school. I'm not pissed, but sometimes I just want to spend a moment or two alone with him in the morning.

7:30 am: Sitting in traffic on I-5 per usual. Ugh! It gets under my skin. I sometimes fear that the angst I build up in the bumper-to-bumper gridlock completely ruins my workday.

10:52 am: Barely been at work for two hours but am already dragging. Maybe it was the particularly crummy traffic this morning. Maybe it's my co-manager, Bruce—he's always micromanaging the team. Or maybe it's just the routine bearing down on me.

2:20 pm: Scrambling to put my PowerPoint together for the 2:30 product meeting. I hate meetings, these in particular. We spend so much time talking on and on—most of my colleagues just love to hear themselves blab. They're caught up in the never-ending battle to please our VP. The meeting hasn't started yet and I'm already upset.

8:05 pm: Just finished the dishes with my husband. I'm tired and have a short fuse. I blew up at my husband for emailing at the table again. I know I overreacted but . . . argh . . . it's just so frustrating. All I want is a little family time to catch up on our day. I want to check in with the kids, to actually hear how things are going at school. I want to check in with him, too. The days just seem to bleed together, one into the next. I just wish I could slow them down and enjoy the ride more.

As you can see, Real-Time Journaling generates a play-by-play of the day's frustrations, its shortcomings. It's definitely useful from a goal-identification standpoint but, as you can see, it's often not the cheeriest process. In order to combat Real-Time Notes' problem-centric tone, we recommend that you regularly practice a gratitude exercise in parallel (Gratitude Journaling is a perfect example). We want you to identify change targets, but not take on a pessimistic or negative outlook. As one of our students once said, "If I only wrote down all the times my boyfriend did something I didn't like for a week, I'd break up with him." Real-Time Notes is not a one-way street to breaking up. Rather, it creates a real-time roadmap of the moments that are undercutting your happiness and meaning and, therefore, performance. When juxtaposed with your vision statement, Real-Time Notes can be a key step in defining your most important change goals.

YOUR GOALS

As we discussed at the beginning of our goals discussion, transitioning to goal-setting marks a significant inflection point in our framework. It is the first step we take from working on self-awareness to pursuing self-commitment. Up until goal identification, the majority of our framework has focused on self-knowing. It's been about growing in our self-awareness and identifying our core values. Now, as we transition to goal identification, it's time to BE. It's time to plan how we want to begin *living* in alignment with our values, our vision, our calling. And, as we alluded to at the beginning of our goals section, transitioning to BE is not easy. It means looking at our current circumstance and admitting shortcomings. It means acknowledging the emptiness, unfulfillment, and or dissatisfaction within. Beginning to BE, whether by going through our or your own transformation goal identification techniques, requires courage and honesty. It requires a true awareness that transcends the pitfalls of your ego, story, thoughts, and emotions—an awareness that you've been cultivating since this book's opening pages.

Now that you have learned several techniques for identifying personal change goals, it's time to put them into action. Whether you use the methods as we've outlined them or prefer to examine the gaps between your current situation and your calling through your own process, it's up to you. What we ask and recommend is that you take enough time to truly think through how best to begin applying your C-V Statement to your current life. Focus on the areas that mean the most to you. If, over the course of your goal-setting process, you begin to hesitate, to feel fear and internal tension over the scale or implications of the goals you're thinking about, please flip back to our "Anticipated Tension" sections. Trust in yourself. Remember, even though it's not easy, Change. Is. Possible. As we've harped on all along, setting change goals requires honesty, self-awareness, and a healthy dose of courage. But don't worry, you'll see in the next chapter that no matter how audacious or difficult your goals appear to be, you will be able to break them down into manageable and compelling chucks that will bring you to successful change outcomes.

With these things in mind, take some time to flush out your most important personal change goals. When you are ready, make a list. Feel free to write several of your main ones here:

Change Goal 1:

_____

_____

Potential Method:

_____

_____

Change Goal 2:

_____

_____

Potential Method:

_____

_____

Change Goal 3:

_____

_____

Potential Method:

_____

_____

THE TOOLS
A SUMMARY

This chapter is all about techniques for goal formation. The three methods we cover extensively are:

1. Miracle and Exception Questions

From solutions-focused brief therapy, the Miracle and Exception Questions allow you to visualize a positive outlier and then think about the last time you experienced that positive outlier in your life. Help show change is possible and helps you establish parameters surround that change.

2. Your Ideal Day

A self-descriptive technique inspired by the book *Tuesdays with Morrie*, this method simply asks you to thoughtfully and with your C-V Statement in hand write down your ideal day. Juxtapose with your current reality and make change goals out of the biggest gaps.

3. Real-Time Notes

From the time you wake up until the time you go to bed, jot down the significant day events and your corresponding emotions. Do this for at least several days in a row. Be honest and insightful. Use as an indicator for what's working and what's not. Create goals accordingly.

NATE'S STATUS UPDATE

With a solid first draft vision statement in hand, Nate began to pursue the goal identification process. He began comparing his current reality with the C-V Statement he had come up with, keeping in mind the tensions people often have with both Tweak and Overhaul goals. We encouraged him not to feel overwhelmed in the face of new change and reminded him that *change is possible*. After thinking on his own for a while, Nate decided to use the Ideal Day exercise to help narrow down some of his most important goals. After plenty of honest self-reflection and quite a bit of discussion, Nate was able to identify the following four top change goals and potential methods. He was ready for change implementation.

Change Goal 1: *Try to use my experience and position at the firm to work on thought-leadership/organizational learning projects that help the company but also contribute to the realm of economic policy as a whole.*

Potential Method: *Come up with a project proposal and ask the CEO and Board for support (concrete idea: begin sending out weekly e-flyer on the topic, start my own blog and get it in front of my company's eyes somehow).*

Change Goal 2: *Increase the sense of cohesion and positivity on my team at work.*

Potential Method: *Teach and encourage team members to use PQ Reps. Do them before team meetings.*

Change Goal 3: *Spend more QUALITY time with Chloe and the children.*

Potential Method: *Come home by 6 pm at least three times a week. Take the children to school at least once a week. Do a random act of kindness for my family once a week.*

Change Goal 4: *Lose 15 lbs. Gain more energy.*

Potential Method: *Run for 40 minutes with Izzie 2–3 times per week (it'll be good for Izzie too).*

CHAPTER 6

Make the Change

LEAD

BE

KNOW

Since the beginning of the book, we've been laying the groundwork for personal transformation. We've examined who we are not by walking through many of our egoic and

Go confidently in the direction of your dreams. Live the life you've imagined."

–Henry David Thoreau

identity pitfalls. We've looked within and strived for greater self-awareness via a variety of proven self-discovery techniques. We've contemplated our core values and drafted our calling in the form of a personal vision statement. And in the previous chapter, we've compared that vision to the reality of our current circumstances, coming up with a prioritized list of personal change goals. The journey through KNOW and the first part of BE has required diligence and commitment. You've dedicated time. You've dedicated energy. You've challenged yourself to truly introspect and to disassociate from the things and impulses that cloud your sense of self. You should be proud of your progress. Thank you for the work you've done thus far. You've brought yourself closer to living your calling and are ready to move forward. Let's move toward change.

THE NATURE OF CHANGE

Before we get into actually implementing change, it's worth discussing the nature of change. As we said in our opening pages, change is hard. Our society abounds with sentiments like "people resist change" or "you can't teach an old dog new tricks." And these feelings and struggles manifest themselves in our own personal experiences. The effects of your company's team-building retreat get lost in day-to-day busy work within days, you abandon your New Year's resolution by March, and your summer weight-loss commitment fizzles as soon as peach cobbler season arrives. Our lives and the lives of the people we know are littered with examples of failed change efforts. As a result, we often become discouraged and skeptical of change. Worst of all, as many of you have experienced, we settle for less; we settle for discontent and unfulfillment.

However, the good news is, and as we've stressed all along, *Change. Is. Possible.* The great news is, for those of you who have taken this journey with us, *change is highly probable*. From the very beginning, we've been doing all of the crucial pre-transformation work that people often miss out on or do incorrectly. We've taken time to self-explore and determine the true nature of our calling. We've set goals that are in alignment with who we are and where we truly want to go. Now, if we can understand the basic parameters surrounding a successful change effort just a little more deeply, we'll be ready to go.

Change is not hard because we lack the initial desire. Change is hard because we don't understand and anticipate our own psychology. We don't understand the pitfalls and tensions that exist within our minds. Many times, we logically want one thing, but emotionally and often subconsciously yearn for something else. How many times have you committed to something but, when the time came to follow through, not really *felt* like it? We're certain you can think of at least several examples. Put most simply, we are not of one mind.

As an illustration, let's say you're the summer dieter mentioned previously. In mid-May, you receive a summer swim catalogue in the mail and you think, *Oh shoot! Summer is coming up around the corner. I want to lose some weight so that I can fit into and enjoy one of these beautiful suits.* As extra motivation, you end up purchasing one of the swimsuits in the catalogue. Due to a high volume of orders (you've selected a very stunning, popular suit), the swimsuit company informs you that your request is backordered and therefore won't arrive until mid-summer. You're a little peeved initially, but after a few moments you look on the bright side and figure that the backorder will just give you more time to get in good shape. The day after placing your order, you embark on a diet. It's nothing too crazy—you're just cutting out desserts and the other sweets you sometimes snack on throughout the day. After four weeks of adhering to this plan, you've lost nine pounds and are feeling much better about your physique and health. You think, *Beach-bod here I come!* But then, temptation strikes. At the end of June, your local market gets its first batch of summer peaches. You absolutely love this juicy, succulent fruit and have built a reputation amongst your friends for making the sweetest peach cobbler and most mouth-watering peach ice cream every summer. You think to yourself, *There's no way I can abandon my love for tasty summer peach desserts.* And then, as an afterthought, *I can make peach cobbler for my friends and family but only eat a little . . .* Lo and behold, you cannot. In the three weeks between your first peach cobbler and your sixth peach cobbler, you end up gaining back six pounds. The swimsuit you ordered, something you had nearly forgotten about, arrives in mid-July, and your physique is nearly back to where it was when you started. *Oh well,* you think to yourself, *there's always next summer;* and you toss the brand new suit, tags still affixed, into the depths of your dresser.

Whether you've ever had a bathing suit weight loss battle or not, you can certainly relate to a scenario where an intended change fell short due to internal opposition. Over the last thirty years, behavioral psychologists have conducted extensive research on the logical-emotional divide that exists within all of us—resulting in a myriad of interesting, ever-evolving findings, descriptions, and analogies. One of our favorite paradigms comes from University of Virginia psychologist Jonathan Haidt in his book, *The Happiness Hypothesis*. Haidt describes the emotional part of us as a gigantic, rumbling elephant, and the logical part of us as a determined, but obviously much smaller, elephant rider.[1] Whenever the rider wants to set off in a given direction, he must cajole and steer the humongous elephant down the appropriate road. In reality, the rider's influence over the elephant is fairly limited and, in cases when the elephant is in disagreement, is completely illusory. The rider can struggle all he wants, he can exhaust himself to his wits' end, but ultimately he'll be forced to go wherever the elephant's traipsing feet carry them. He is no match. However, when the rider and the elephant are motivated in the same direction, all the rider has to do is hold on and make minor, well-informed adjustments along the way. The going is easy, powerful, and effective.

We love this paradigm because it is so easy to apply it to the change efforts we've all experienced. When we attempt a change and our logical rider and emotional elephant powerhouse are in alignment, we succeed wonderfully. On the other hand, when our rider and elephant disagree, we experience internal turmoil and then our elephant reigns supreme. It's not easy to admit, but our self-control, our rider's wrangling, is exhaustible. It's a fact that has been proven over and over again in psychology and in many of our personal experiences. At work, even though your rider has made a commitment to start being more patient and understanding of the people you manage, in high-stress situations your elephant still spurs you to make sarcastic comments and public callouts. Despite your plan to quit smoking over four weeks, the tumultuousness of your relationship five weeks from now sends you scurrying down to 7-Eleven on the back of your elephant for another pack. In the previous peach cobbler example, your weight-loss commitment goes by the wayside once the elephant within you sees the pretty peaches down another road and charges off in that direction.

For simple yet scientific evidence of how this logical–emotional tug of war and the subsequent self-control drain is intrinsic to all of us, we need look no further than the realm of four-year-olds. In 1970, Stanford University psychologist Walter Mischel and his team of researchers conducted what is now affectionately dubbed the "Stanford marshmallow experiment."[2] In the experiment, the researchers would bring a preschool child, ranging in age from four to six, into a small room and let him or her play with toys for a little while. After a few minutes, the researcher would offer the child a treat, frequently a marshmallow. The researcher would then explain that he had to step out of the room for a few minutes, but would leave the one marshmallow with the child. He told the child that he or she was free to eat the one marshmallow any time they wanted but that if they resisted until he returned, they would get to enjoy two marshmallows. The results were simultaneously adorable and, more importantly, telling.[3] Of the over 600 children that went through Mischel's study, the average participant resisted for less than three minutes before caving in and eating the single marshmallow. For all of the children, even the minority that succeeded in waiting the nearly fifteen minutes it took for the researcher to return with two marshmallows, there was a lot of squirming, hungering, and staring along the way. For a few, their young riders were so ineffective that they gobbled down the single marshmallow right away.

As you can see, logical–emotional tension exists within all of us, beginning at the early stages of childhood and continuing through-out our adult lives. What does this mean for our impending change efforts? It means that, in order to successfully implement change, we must address both our rider and our elephant (Figure 14).

FIGURE 14

If we're the children in the marshmallow experiment we just described, we must logically set the goal of two marshmallows and then emotionally motivate ourselves toward the double sugary deliciousness provided by those two marshmallows. Or, in other words, we must align our internal selves with our desired external world. Our intellect, our emotions, our passions, our environment, and our direction must all be aligned in order to successfully undergo personal transformation. As we said at the beginning, you achieve the Inside-Out Effect by living your life—both professionally and personally—in alignment with who you truly are. You achieve it by discovering the core values and true self within and then living each day in the direction that they point. Doing so minimizes internal friction, and optimizes your energy around that which matters most—living with a sense of purpose, fulfillment, and happiness.

The good news for us is, though we haven't been explicitly discussing the human brain's logical rider–emotional elephant bifurcation throughout the book, we have set ourselves up for success all along. **Helping you implement actual change in your lives is the most crucial step of our entire framework.** As such, from the get-go, we've been laying the foundation for a successful personal transformation effort. We've been targeting the *right* goals by looking *within ourselves* for the things that most inspire and resonate with us, rather than *outside ourselves*. We've crafted a C-V Statement that is both emotionally inspirational and logically concrete. We've anticipated and overcome some of the big tensions surrounding our goals—freeing ourselves from some of our initial, gut-check fear and, hopefully, lowering our inner resistance as we approach change. Now it's time to take that step. It's time to commit to change.

OUR CHANGE AGENT: RITUALS

Though over the course of this transformation process we've begun striving for greater awareness of ourselves and the world around us, so much of what we still do on a daily basis is done routinely. It's done habitually. The way you brush your teeth at the beginning and end of each day (at least, we hope you do), the drive you take to work each morning, the way you run team meetings, the fact that you read the paper while you eat lunch, and your consistent nightly shower are all part of this routine, this daily habit. Psychologists have come to classify these habits—these routine thoughts and actions—as automatic processes. Automatic processes do not require conscious thought, are constantly executing in parallel, and occur within our brains thousands of times a day. Though very useful for helping us manage our complex and busy lives, they are one of the biggest obstacles to successful change implementation. This is because, as consistently executed thoughts and behaviors, automatic processes are implicitly endorsed by our elephants. They are so engrained in our daily routine that they are effortless. On the

> First we make our habits,
> then our habits make us."
> –Charles C. Noble

day that we decide to begin transforming our behavior, we're forced to dedicate conscious thought and active energy to a part of our routine we don't normally think about. We have to apply effort to a formerly effortless process. Here comes tension. All of a sudden our rider is nudging our elephant off of the traditionally followed road and, if we haven't prepared adequately, is going to struggle to do so. In order to avoid this struggle (and eventual failure from exhaustion), it's crucial that we pursue change in a way that minimizes the long-run tension with our automatic processes.

Although at first glance this may seem impossible, the solution for successful change is to form new automatic processes. We always tell our clients, *the best way to enact change in your life, the best way to begin living your calling, is by learning how to build and implement rituals based on your goals.* By rituals we mean carefully and compellingly designed, repeatable behaviors that you integrate into your life on a regular basis. In contrast to attempts at one-time comprehensive changes or vaguely defined incremental changes, which require constant active thought and self-control, rituals pull us toward change. They pull us because they are compelling; they are specific; and they are repeatable. Above all else, rituals pull us because, when implemented successfully over time, they become habits; they become frictionless automatic processes that appeal to both our elephants and riders and are intrinsic parts of our daily routine.

Through rituals, we can break down all of our goals, regardless of whether they're Overhaul or Tweak Goals, into manageable parts. We make these parts compelling and meaningful. We then repeat these parts over and over to the point that they become default steps in our daily routine. Then we proceed to the next manageable part. Over time, this system pulls us toward our goals, constantly bringing us into greater alignment with our calling. Allow us to show you how to make rituals that work.

Brain Bite
Rituals and Neuroplasticity[4]

Not long ago, the widely held belief was that our brains were hardwired at birth to function in a series of predetermined ways. They were seen as complex mazes of immutable neural connections. However, over the last several decades, neuroscientists have discovered that our brains are not hardwired. They are actually quite plastic, able to be rewired over time.

The brain's ability to structurally rewire itself is called neuroplasticity. In layman's terms, neuroplasticity can be explained by the phrase "cells that fire together, wire together" (known in the neuroscience community as the Hebbian Principle). Any time we learn something new or do a behavior for the first time, neurons (the brain's building block cells) make new connections with other neurons. A neuron makes a new connection or "fires" with another neuron by sending a chemical neurotransmitter across the gap between them called a synapse. As a behavior is repeated or a set of knowledge is revisited, the neurons that fired together the first time fire together again. Much like how muscle tissue strengthens when lifting weights, every time a set of neurons fire together, their connection gets stronger. In neurobiological terms, the electrochemical relationship between neurons is reconfigured—more neurotransmitters gather on the sending side of the synapse and the voltage is increased on the receiving side to attract more neurotransmitters. This strengthening between neurons over time is called long-term potentiation.

Long-term potentiation is the key to creating new endur-ing neural pathways (new long-term memories), and it is ex-actly what happens when we successfully implement rituals. Day 1 of a ritual is often the first time a given series of neurons have fired together. In order to engrain a ritual within the fabric of our daily lives, we must consciously and resiliently do it over and over again. Over time, the neural pathway as-sociated with that ritual will reach long-term potentiation. When that happens, the effort required to carry out the ritual is significantly less. Not only have you formed a new habit, you've successfully changed the structure of your brain!

RITUAL STEP I: ROADMAP THE RIDER

The first step in ritual formation is to make sure your ritual is (1) accurate and (2) clear. On the accuracy front, it should fit cleanly in line with your overall transformation goal; it should be a logical and meaningful step toward your calling. As for clarity, you want to give your rider explicit direction for where to redirect the elephant. Be specific. Here are some things to consider.

The Work We've Already Done

The good news for this step is that we've already laid an incred-ibly strong foundation in KNOW and the first two chapters of BE. In KNOW, we spent an extensive amount of time contem-plating the nature of our calling by pursuing the answer to the ques-tion "who am I?" After starting with techniques for improving our self-awareness, we then took the next step by articulating our core values and drafting a C-V Statement. We then, throughout the last two chapters, anticipated some of our tensions and plunged into the goal identification process. The result of our honesty, courage, and intense introspection during these two parts is that we have a quality roadmap to give our rider. We're not chasing something that won't fulfill us; we aren't mistaking who we are for who we are not. We have a list of transformation goals and they are true; they resonate and are aligned with our core selves. Lean on the wisdom you built up over the preceding parts of this framework to guide you in articulating what your rituals should be. Look at the transformation goals and potential methods you wrote down at the end of last chapter. Your rituals are right there. All you have to do is uncover and fine-tune them.

(Note: If for some reason you haven't yet identified your change goals, please turn back to the end of the last chapter and do so now. The remainder of this chapter will be significantly more meaningful if you do.)

Language

In their book, *The Three Laws of Performance*, Steve Zaffron and Dave Logan unveil their Second Law of Performance as "How a situation occurs arises in language." They say, "Language is the means through which your future is already written. It is also the means through which it can be rewritten."[5] We agree wholeheartedly. How you word your ritual and the specifics you choose to include are incredibly important. Do you word it in a way that, as we previously said, is consistent with your ultimate change goal? Is the connection obvious? Does the language you use pull at you? Does it give crystal clear direction while still motivating you? Think about the way you word your ritual. It can be the difference between successfully seeing change through and abandoning it halfway.

Write It Down

Write down your rituals. Post them in a place where you'll see them regularly. Though this point may seem intuitive, it's extremely important and often overlooked. By simply writing a ritual down, you're more likely to remember it because you've interacted with it in another medium (beyond just speaking or thinking it). When you write rituals and goals down, not only do you remember them better, you also achieve them

> "Watch your thoughts, for they become your words. Watch your words, for they become your actions. Watch your actions, for they become your habits. Watch your habits, for they become your character. Watch your character, for it becomes your destiny."
> —*Unknown*

more often. A study done by Gail Matthews, a professor of psychology at Dominican University, shows that people who write down their goals are nearly 40% more successful in achieving them than people who don't.[6] This is because when we write our rituals down and keep them in a visible place, we end up revisiting them more often. We see them as we brush our teeth or make our morning toast and remember our commitment. Our odds of following through go up substantially (amazingly, research done by Dave Kohl, professor emeritus at Virginia Tech, indicates that less than 1% of Americans write down and review their goals on a regular basis). So please, beyond writing your rituals down, put them in a visible place. Post them somewhere where you'll see them several times a day. Tape them to your bathroom mirror, put them on your screen saver, on your smartphone wallpaper, or keep them on your kitchen table. Do whatever it takes to ensure that you see them regularly. When you do, they will stare you in the face and hold you accountable. They will be constant sources of crystal clear direction that keep you heading in the right direction; they'll keep you heading toward your calling.

RITUAL STEP II: SPUR THE ELEPHANT

As we've discussed throughout this chapter, **the elephant is the biggest factor in whether or not we successfully change our lives.** As our emotional center, our elephant is the part

> "There's no passion to be found in playing small—in settling for a life that is less than the one you are capable of living."
>
> –Nelson Mandela

of us that often resists the cajoling of our riders, the part of us that stubbornly fights to keep the status quo, to adhere to our long-built-up automatic processes. If we don't adequately motivate the elephant within us, our rituals may start strongly but will ultimately stagnate and fail. Though all of us have a deep-rooted emotional connection to the way *things are*, the good news is, as we've uncovered throughout KNOW, we have an even deeper-rooted emotional connection to the way *we'd like things to be.* Thus, the key to our success is being able to create compelling rituals that help us consistently remember and draw on this burning motivation within us. As the world-famous motivator Tony Robbins says, "There is a powerful, driving force inside every human being that, once unleashed, can make any vision, dream, or desire a reality." We must unleash and sustain that force through each of our rituals. Here are some of the most important ways to do it.

Compelling Vision, Revisited

In the last chapter of KNOW, you crafted your C-V Statement using the C3PO Rule (Clear, Compelling, Concise, Present Tense, Others). In so doing, you balanced concreteness with loftiness, implementation with inspiration. The concrete elements of your vision are extremely important because, as we've said, they help roadmap your rider. However, your vision's enduring power lies in its compelling qualities—for these motivate your elephant. Based on your core values and true self, your vision's compelling elements outweigh your elephant's default, status quo motivation and spurs it toward change. Look back at your C-V Statement. Which parts of it contain the fire within you? Which parts resonate so powerfully that they almost seem to pull you toward change? Which parts would, if you can imagine yourself in a moment of weakness, snap you back into the direction you want to go? These parts, these sentiments and ideas, need to find their way into your rituals. They are what compel you toward transformation. Harness their power in the new habits you're working to create.

Support Group

Just as some of you turned to others for feedback in KNOW, it is *extremely* effective to ask others to actively support you in your change efforts. Though it's fairly obvious that having a caring support group can be instrumental to achievement, recovery, healing, and change in general, we all too often fail to form one when we're undergoing change. Whether it's because we feel guilty inconveniencing people, don't make the time, or subconsciously prefer not to make one so that we don't let anyone down when we fail, enlisting the help of those who care about us is often something we kick to the curb. Don't make that mistake. Find people, similar to those you might have asked for authentic feedback in KNOW (in fact, if you used the authentic feedback method in KNOW, we highly recommend you ask those people to be your support group), to support and check in on you over the course of your change process. The quantity of your supporters is far less important than the quality of your supporters. Whoever you choose, whether it's just a colleague and your spouse or it's a list of your eight most trusted mentors and friends, make sure that they understand what you're trying to accomplish. Give them a copy of your goals and rituals. Let them know where you see yourself now and where you intend to go. Most of all, ask them if you can come to them in times of crisis. All change efforts experience turbulence. When your elephant starts rumbling, you want to be able to turn to them for reassurance, inspiration, and steadfast support.

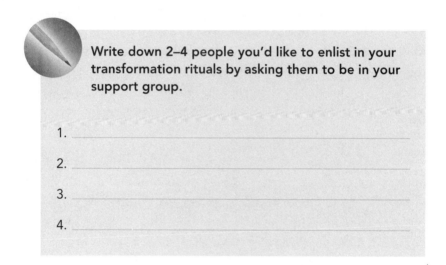

Write down 2–4 people you'd like to enlist in your transformation rituals by asking them to be in your support group.

1. _____

2. _____

3. _____

4. _____

Face the Fear

One of our biggest asks of you throughout this process has been courage. Courage to honestly introspect. Courage to ask yourself the hard questions. Courage to earnestly engage with the answers, even if they're difficult. The reason that we call on courage so emphatically is because most of us feel fear when we pursue change—and we feel it strongly.

Fear, in and of itself, is not an evil or useless emotion. Rooted in the survivalist instincts of our basest hindbrain, fear kept our ancient ancestors from hunting too close to the lion pride or from treading to close to the cliff edge. These days, it teaches children not to touch the hot stove or to be careful when attempting to body surf ten-foot waves (a lesson a young Michael learned firsthand). However, in today's society, fear is often misappropriated. It is too widespread. When our riders attempt to direct our elephants down a new road, they all too often panic. Not only do we fear the hot stove, we fear trying something new. Not only do we fear skydiving, we fear putting ourselves out there at work. In today's world, we not only fear the things that are guaranteed or have a high probability of harming us, we often fear anything that has even the slightest chance of making us uncomfortable, embarrassed, or struggle in any way. We don't express our opinion in meetings, we don't ask our teammates for honest feedback, and we don't have that salary conversation with our boss.

This isn't to say that we're all a bunch of wimps who never stick up for ourselves—we certainly do on occasion. Yet many times, especially when it comes to enacting change in our lives, we can be paralyzed by fear. When we attempt to transform ourselves, we're bombarded by questions like *What if I fail? Am I good enough? How can I ever see this through?* We think about our futures and as we let uncertainty crawl into the picture, we begin to worry; we become nervous; we start to second guess. However, if you remember back to the first part of KNOW, this whirlpool of self-doubt is not intrinsically linked to who we are. These negative thoughts and emotions are identity pitfalls generated by the voice inside our heads; they are generated by our egos. For our egos, anything that stands a chance to diminish us, anything that could potentially put a chink in the armor it has tirelessly forged, is a serious threat and should be avoided. Enter: fear. Fortunately, we can make a different choice. In our awareness, we can acknowledge and then dismiss the voice in our heads and pursue that which matters most to us: lasting fulfillment and performance.

> " Courage is simply the willingness to be afraid and act anyway."
> –Robert Anthony

Of course, just because we have cultivated our awareness and are able to disassociate from the pitfalls of our egos, it doesn't mean that we won't hesitate along the way. Depending on the magnitude and nature of our change goals, we will definitely encounter friction and fear as we pursue them. However, if we trust the goals and rituals we lay out for ourselves as well as have courage, we will persevere and get closer to our calling. As Steve Jobs said to a bunch of wide-eyed, whole-world-ahead-of-them Stanford grads in 2005, "Believing that the dots will connect down the road will give you the confidence to follow your heart even when it leads you off the well-worn path, and that will make all the difference."[7] No matter the stage of life you find yourself in, you are alive and the world is waiting. Don't let fear hijack your opportunity to enhance your circumstance.

About the Authors: Michael's Courage Journey

I have been a pretty positive, optimistic person ever since I was a little kid. As much as I'd like to attribute it to nature, a lot of it was certainly nurture. I grew up with extremely supportive parents who told me since my earliest days, "You can be and do whatever you set your mind to, Mikey." And when they said it, they meant it. They said it when I was four and aspired to be a zebra. They said it when I was twelve and wanted to play in the NBA. They said it when I was nineteen and wanted to be a venture capitalist. No matter the goal or the dream, they supported me genuinely.

As I grew up, however, I learned that the majority of society did not share my parents' attitude. In society's eyes, an eleven-year-old who wanted to be a professional athlete was cute, but a high schooler who had the same stated goal was out of his mind. I learned that society, that is, the collective us, likes to take other people's audacious dreams and respond with a resounding "Yeah, riiiiight." We look at ourselves as pragmatists. We pride ourselves on injecting "realism" into edgy or out-of-the-norm aspirations. We like to bring each other back down to earth.

Yet, as time went by, I realized that society wasn't bringing me back down to earth; it was just bringing me down. It was burying me beneath the weight of caution, the weight of fear. I felt it and I didn't want to be buried. I didn't want to wait around for society to censor me into an acceptable profession or lifestyle. I wanted to pursue a life that invigorated me, that resonated and had meaning. So, during my first week of college, I printed out a quote that inspired me and taped it to my dorm room wall. It was a variation of a very famous quote originally written by Marianne Williamson.[8] It reads:

Our deepest fear is not that we are inadequate. Our deepest fear is that we are powerful beyond measure. It is our light, not our darkness, that most frightens us. Your playing small does not serve the world. There is nothing enlightened about shrinking so that other people won't feel insecure around you. We were all meant to shine as children do. It's not just in some of us; it is in everyone. And as we let our own lights shine, we unconsciously give other people permission to do the same. As we are liberated from our own fear, our presence automatically liberates others.

Having felt fear try to creep in and curb my search for what would give me meaning, I turned to this quote. Every year, as I moved around campus I would take it off one wall and re-tape it to the next. This quote, on its now faded and tattered piece of paper, now hangs in my home. It is taped to the wall above my desk and is a constant source of my courage. It reminds me, especially in the moments where I feel fear and hesitation attempt to slow my progress toward my calling, that overcoming fear allows us to unleash our true potential, to pursue our goals, and to give hope to others. When we show courage, we begin differentiating ourselves from the "Yeah riiiiight" chorus around us. We begin empowering other people to discover their own courage and seek their calling. "As we are liberated from our own fear, our presence automatically liberates others."

Anticipate the Journey

Another important step in spurring your elephant toward change is being able to help it anticipate the journey. Doing so effectively will enable you to precondition your elephant to what lies ahead and help minimize the chance that it goes charging back to your old habits and ways of doing things when the going gets rough. Specifically, you should anticipate the journey with three things: (1) Visualization, (2) Energy Management, and (3) Action Triggers.

1. Visualization

Visualization is a straightforward but powerful way to help you anticipate the journey. Rather than getting caught up in the initial phases of a new ritual, visualization forces you to embark with the beginning, middle, and end in mind. As you set out on a new change goal by beginning a new ritual, practice visualizing yourself doing that ritual tomorrow, next week, and next month. Visualize how you will continue your ritual through difficult moments.

Given the ritual you're targeting, what do you anticipate are going to be your biggest challenges? Focus in on those challenges and visualize how you will respond in those moments. Visualize your fortitude. What are you going to do or tell yourself in the moments that your elephant's old habits want to take over?

Visualization has a long tradition of helping people with sustained peak performance. One of our colleagues, Dr. Leonard Lane, is the Group Director of Leadership Development at Li & Fung Limited, an international trading group, and is a steadfast proponent of the power of visualization. In addition to using it regularly with the powerful leadership development work he does, he uses it in his personal life as well. He credits his success in the Hawaii Ironman Triathlon to the detailed visualization he did beforehand:

As I approached the Hawaii Ironman, my coach insisted that I clearly visualize what I wanted to feel like at the end of each event. He stressed that I needed to envision as much detail as I could—to see the transitions in my mind. He wanted me to describe exactly what I wanted to feel like at the end of the swim as I transitioned to the bike. Likewise, I needed to see exactly how I would feel as I transitioned from the bike to the run. How did I see myself crossing the finish line?

On the day of the event, I had an incredibly strong mental image of how I was going to carry myself throughout the race. And it's a good thing I did because I was tested on every leg. During the swim, I got a cramp and needed to be pulled up by a lifeguard to have the cramp stretched out. However, due to my focused state of mind, I was able to quickly get back in the water and finish at a good pace. Just as I had envisioned, I transitioned to the bike with confidence, completely letting go of the cramp. I shot out of the transition corral with a burst

*of speed and was off on my bike—my strongest event. As I
zoomed toward the end of the ride, suddenly a 40–50 knot
crosswind knocked me off of my bike and onto the pavement.
A little scratched and shaken up, I clung to my clear vision of
what I wanted to feel like at the end of this leg and I forced
myself to remount and finish with determination. I then transitioned to the last leg: the run. Half way through this leg, the
sun went down and darkness set in. This tends to be discour-
aging for a lot of competitors, but it wasn't for me because
I had already pictured how I wanted to finish the race. As I
had already envisioned, I reached deep within for my reserve
strength and pushed through the rest of the race despite the
setbacks I experienced on each leg. As I crossed the line, I
threw my arms in the air—just as I had planned. I was elated.
I had done it.*

2. Energy Management

Another important component of anticipating the journey is to
manage your energy as you implement your rituals. As we've
touched on throughout the book, change requires effort and energy. Your rider's best intentions and strongest desires for change
are fatigable and can collapse if the task is too tall. Thus, a key
element of spurring your elephant is slotting your rituals into logical and well-spaced times throughout your day. If you get up and
try to crank out your four rituals every morning before breakfast,
odds are you will end up depleting your energy, fatiguing your
rider, and leaving yourself at the mercy of your old habits. Instead,
fit them into a variety of slots; build a rhythm.

Beyond strategically spacing out your rituals throughout the
day, we also recommend that you strategically space out your
timeline for implementing new rituals. By that we mean don't try

to start half-a-dozen news rituals in the same week. Instead, stagger them. For instance, at the very beginning, start with two rituals. Have one of the rituals be one that you can see yourself easily forming into a habit—one that will give you some early confidence and show you that change is possible—and have the other be a more substantive one that targets one of your bigger change goals. After two weeks of doing these first two rituals every day (we *highly* recommend that you check them off on your calendar or some kind of personal list every time you do them), begin your third and fourth rituals, and so on. Depending on how many rituals you've identified, implement them in pairs every two to three weeks. This way, you'll not only build your change effort at a manageable, focused pace, but you'll also gain confidence along the way.

3. Action Triggers

The last and probably most powerful part of anticipating the journey comes through action triggers. Truly in the vein of anticipating your own psychology, forming action triggers is all about explicitly changing your environment in support of your change effort. Here's a common action trigger example: Let's say you want to start exercising in the morning before work. Beyond simply committing to waking up earlier, setting your alarm, and motivating yourself with a five-week weight-loss goal (all good things, by the way), you can anticipate the journey by putting your running shoes and clothes right next to your bed. That way, your gear is waiting for you, almost staring you in the face, when you wake up—a perfect action trigger that will spur you on even if the sleepy side of your elephant puts up a fight.

Action triggers can take a wide range of shapes depending on the rituals you're trying to implement. Wear a bracelet that reminds you to do a certain ritual. Change the way your desk is laid out. Put something inspiring on your screensaver. Clean out the snack drawer at home. Have a colleague remind you to start team meetings a certain way. Action triggers are all about optimizing the world around you to support what you're trying to accomplish. They're particularly effective when you create them around potential relapse areas—areas where you can anticipate your elephant trying to run out of control at a future, less motivated time (moments you can potentially see as you visualize). Get creative with your action triggers. Anticipate your own psychology. With action triggers, you can be your own best friend; you look out for yourself on the journey to change and greatly improve your odds of success.

Brain Bite
The Power of Anticipating the Journey

As we said in the previous Brain Bite about rituals and neuroplasticity, the goal of ritual formation is to create new long-term memories in your brain through reaching long-term potentiation along new neural pathways. Here's how the three "Anticipating the Journey" techniques help with that process:

1. *Visualization*: Contemporary research has shown that simply visualizing an action activates the same neural region that is activated when the action is actually performed. Though the activation generally isn't as strong, it still occurs. Thus, visualization can help solidify new neural pathways and can only help in the journey toward long-term potentiation.[9]

2. *Energy Management*: A very important factor in creating long-term memory is taking an appropriate and consistent amount of time between your rituals. If you do your ritual repeatedly within a short amount of time (something neuroscientists call "massed training"), you will build a robust short-term memory, but ineffective long-term memory (and therefore no new habits). Spacing out your ritual in repeatable intervals will allow time for your brain to create and utilize new neurons, not simply strengthen the ones already made, which leads to the formation of long-term memory. Spacing out your ritual intervals allows your mind to do what's necessary to move toward long-term potentiation.[10]

3. *Action Triggers*: Converting short-term memory into long-term memory is very complex and is highly regulated. Day to day and moment to moment, the brain receives hundreds of millions of bits of information from all of its senses, both externally and internally. Sensory information is first received and interpreted in the primary sensory areas, then sent to unimodal association areas, and it is finally processed in multimodal association areas. Information bits from the environment are first received individually and then processed with each other in the multimodal areas. Our brain aggregates and escalates this data into more complete information at each state until it can understand a comprehensive event. In any memory situation, your brain is taking all the information around you and within you,

like the lighting, noise, social context, your mood, hunger, thirst, attention, etc., and first processing this information individually then bringing it together into something that we can call an event. As one can imagine, this information is quite detailed. The neurons that comprise these event memories receive highly specific information and forge highly specific relationships to one another. As we mentioned in our neuroplasticity Brain Bite, long-term potentiation is reached by neurons repeatedly firing together in a given relationship ("cells that fire together wire together"). The less their relationship is changed, the quicker they can reach long-term potentiation. Thus, from an action trigger standpoint, you can facilitate quicker long-term memory formation by repeating your rituals in a consistent environment with a consistent trigger each time. This will ensure that the event aggregation neural processes and the subsequent neuron relationships are as consistent as possible over time.[11]

A Sense of Urgency

In the twenty-five years of work Behnam has done helping large companies and organizations transform themselves, one of the biggest things he has learned is how crucial it is that they act with a sense of urgency. Far too often he's seen companies' best transformation intentions laid to waste due to indecision and failure to act quickly enough. Employees get disenchanted, leadership gets distracted, and pretty soon, everyone (and their elephants) would rather keep things the same than implement slow and seemingly ineffective change. As it turns out, the same principle holds true when we try to enact change in our own lives. If we move slowly, without urgency, we become complacent and eventually turn to the "there's always next month or next year or next decade" change mantra. That's why, despite the tension that change sometimes presents, we must move forward with a sense of urgency. It's one of the most crucial aspects of spurring our elephant. The time to pursue change is *now*. Not tomorrow, not next week or next year. Now.

Of course, this doesn't mean that you have to completely transform your life in the next five hours; it doesn't mean that you have to rush through your rituals and goals. As we've already discussed, personal change takes methodical time, it takes turning rituals into habits, and it's achieved by striving for incremental wins. However, don't confuse this incremental process with complacency or apathy. Change happens when we are engaged, when we are living as if we have some skin in the game. In fact, if we're honest with ourselves, we always have skin in the game. Our skin. Our life. To hammer this point home, let us turn to one of the greatest Stanford commencement addresses by one of the greatest entrepreneurs and visionaries of our time, Mr. Steve Jobs.

> . . . *My third story is about death. When I was seventeen, I read a quote that went something like "if you live each day as if it was your last, someday you'll most certainly be right." It made an impression on me and since then, for the past thirty-three years, I've looked in the mirror every morning and asked myself, "If today were the last day of my life, would I want to do what I'm about to do today?" Whenever the answer has been "no" for too many days in a row, I know I need to change something. Remembering that I'll be dead soon*

is the most important tool I've ever encountered to help me make the big choices in life. Because almost everything, all external expectations, all pride, all fear of embarrassment or failure, these things just fall away in the face of death, leaving what is truly important. Remembering that you are going to die is the best way I know of to think that you have nothing to lose. You are already naked. There is no reason not to follow your heart . . .

After recounting how he had been diagnosed with pancreatic cancer the year prior and how, against all odds, had a rare form that was curable with surgery, Steve continues:

This was the closest I've been to facing death and I hope it's the closest I get for a few more decades. Having lived through it, I can now say this to you with a bit more certainty than when death was a useful but purely intellectual concept: no one wants to die. Even people who want to go to heaven don't want to die to get there. And yet, death is the destination we all share. No one has ever escaped it. And that is as it should be, because death is the single best invention of life. It's life's change agent. It clears out the old to make way for the new. Right now, the new is you, but some day, not too long from now, you will gradually become the old and be cleared away. Sorry to be so dramatic but it's quite true. Your time is limited so don't waste it living someone else's life. Don't be trapped by dogma, which is living with the results of other people's thinking. Don't let the noise of others' opinions drown out your own inner voice. And most important, have the courage to follow your heart and intuition—they somehow already know what you truly want to become. Everything else is secondary.[12]

Steve's words that day were simultaneously simple and powerful. They are emotive and bittersweet. As most of you probably know, Steve passed away in October 2011, finally succumbing to the cancer he fought for eight years. He never got the "few more decades" he hoped for, but we can be sure that he lived the extra time he had as if it really counted. He was a man who was in touch with who he truly was and what truly mattered to him. He aligned what he did with who he was; he spent his life living his calling and living inside-out. All the while, he motivated himself—created a sense of urgency in his life—by remembering that his time on this earth was limited and, therefore, precious. It's a lesson that we all could get better at internalizing. And now, as we strive to transform our lives, is a lesson that we should carry especially close. We must inject urgency into our rituals. The time for change is *now*. We only get one life. Make the moments count.

A Man Who Found His Urgency[13]

From the depths of one of America's deepest tragedies, Ney Melo was able to find the sense of urgency he needed to change his life. He was able to discover a new passion, a new career, and the woman of his dreams.

Raised in New York City, Ney Melo was always a hard worker. He was born to an immigrant family and was taught from an early age that working diligently in school was the path to a greater life and success. After years of hitting the books as a kid, Ney's efforts were rewarded when he received a scholarship to the selective Regis High School in Manhattan. Fast-forward a handful of years and Ney went on to graduate college with an accounting degree and eventually land a job with the, at the time, highly prestigious world-wide investment bank Lehman Brothers. As Ney says when recounting that part of his life, "This was a success."

On the morning of September 11, 2001, Ney was at his Lehman Brothers office in lower Manhattan when he and his co-workers heard a loud noise and rumble. They ran to their 24th floor window and looked across the street. There they saw a gigantic fiery hole in the World Trade Center's North Tower. The first plane, American Airlines Flight 11, had just crashed into the building. The terrorist attacks of 9/11 had begun. Almost immediately, Ney and his co-workers headed for the elevators. Ney recounts:

> *"There was an elevator open and I remember being in this elevator going down. My mind started racing through my life . . . I thought, 'If I ever get out of here alive, I'm never doing this job again.'"*

Fortunately, Ney did make it out of the elevator and survived the September 11th terrorist attacks. In the days following 9/11, he felt restless and needed to distract himself from all that was going on around him. In Ney's words, he "needed something just to keep busy." His outlet came surprisingly. One day, Ney saw an advertisement for tango class and decided to sign up. He began by committing for just a few weeks, but after learning the basics he began to enjoy it more with each passing day and class. Pretty soon he found himself signing up month after month. He had become a self-described "tango addict."

As it turns out for Ney, love comes in pairs. During one of his first few tango classes, as he was still honing his basic skills, he approached a beautiful woman and asked her to dance. She described it as follows: "I remember this new person coming up and introducing himself to me and asking me to dance. And I could tell that he was a beginner; he didn't have a lot of technique. But I could tell he was going to be good by the way he embraced me."

The woman's name was Jennifer Bratt, and she is now, 10 years later, Ney's dance partner as well as life partner. They share a passion for tango and have even fostered each other's dreams by pursuing it together as a career. The two of them are now professional tango dancers who travel the world teaching, choreographing, and learning more tango. They periodically visit Argentina (the birthplace of tango) to explore their passion for the dance together. Beyond tango, Ney and Jennifer are preparing to share an expanded family as Jennifer is expecting twins.

Ney says, "When I think back 10 years ago, if someone had told me that I'd be doing tango and travelling around the world, I would have thought they were crazy." He realizes that he didn't commit to living his life on his own terms, living his own passion and calling, until he was able to grasp just how short that life is. "The events of 9/11 were the catalyst for the changes I made in my life," he recalls. By witnessing the impermanence of life, Ney decided to start living. He created his own urgency. And in so doing, he discovered his wife, his children, his calling, and his happiness.

Brain Bite
Spur the Elephant[14]

There are strong neurological underpinnings as to why spurring the elephant is an important part of ritual formation, and they revolve around the functions of the brain's limbic system. Anatomically, the limbic system sits atop the brain stem and underneath the cerebral cortex (think middle of the brain). It is in charge of two very important functions: emotional expression and memory formation. The limbic system's substructure, the amygdala, is particularly relevant.

The amygdala is one of our brain's biggest emotional response centers. It is especially responsible for strong feelings related to survival such as fear, anger, and sexuality. The amygdala also plays an important role in long-term memory formation. It helps determine how and where given memories are stored. These dual functions of the amygdala are precisely why spurring the elephant is so important neurologically. Researchers have found that the amount of emotion-based activity in the amygdala at the time of memory formation has a significant impact on the strength and retention of that memory. Translation: The greater the amount of emotional weight ascribed to a new activity, the greater the chance that that activity is retained as habit long term.

Spur that elephant. It will provide sustained meaning to the rituals you're trying to implement, and it'll make your brain a stronger ally, too.

PUTTING IT ALL TOGETHER

Now that we've walked through the key components of ritual formation, it's time to put them all together. Remember, rituals work because they are incremental, repeatable, clear, and compelling. They are formulated in such a way that they anticipate our own mental breakdowns and relapses so that we can catch ourselves when we might otherwise slip back into old behaviors or shy away from change. When done daily for over two months, rituals become habits.[15] They become easier. They move from controlled to routine thought—becoming part of our automatic processes. The following is the standard format we use for writing down rituals, as well as one of Nate's rituals as an example. As you can see, our ritual format entails every change element we've

> I hear and I forget. I see and I remember. I do and I understand."
> –Confucius

just touched on. It includes roadmapping your rider and spurring your elephant. It asks you to anticipate the journey and to tie it to your calendar. We encourage you to use this format (or something similar) to write down your own rituals.

Ritual Format

Ritual (frequency, clarity): _____

Target Goal: _____

Why It Matters/Tie to Vision and Values: _____

Anticipate the Journey: _____

Date Initiated: _____

-Pull your elephant quote-

Nate—RITUAL 1

Ritual: *Come home by 6 pm on Mondays, Wednesdays, and Fridays*

Target Goal: *Spend more QUALITY time with Chloe and the children*

Why It Matters/Tie to Vision: *I know that, at my core, I want to make time for the things that mean the most to me on a regular basis and family is definitely one of my core values. As I've laid out in my C-V Statement: "I will spend time with my children, be present in their lives, and create irreplaceable memories with them. I will communicate openly, honestly, and most importantly, from a place of love with Chloe. I will appreciate her everyday."*

Anticipate the Journey: *Set an alarm on my phone that goes off at 5:15 pm on each of those days. Have Marci, my assistant at work, come to my office at 5:20 on those days. Give her permission to "kick me out."*

Start Date: *Next week (April 14).*

Pull My Elephant: *My children are growing up—they'll be off to college before I know it. My time with them is precious. Don't waste it on an extra Excel spreadsheet. At the end of my life, I will certainly cherish a family game of Taboo over an end-of-day client call.*

While, as we laid out in KNOW, an important part of finding greater meaning and performance in your life is being more aware and appreciative of the routine things that we regularly cruise by on autopilot, it's also important to acknowledge and understand the building blocks of our psychology. It's important to acknowledge the rider-elephant dichotomy within each of us. It's important to acknowledge the fact that our self-control is fatigable. And it is important to acknowledge that much of what we do each day is done as part of a habit-backed routine. When we recognize these facts about our fundamental psychology and the way we behave, we put ourselves at a huge advantage for successfully implementing change in our lives. We put ourselves in the position to become ritual-making experts. It is now time to build that expertise. It's time to make your own rituals. It's time for you to begin transforming your life. So, please, take a few hours to look over your goals and potential methods that you made at the end of the last chapter and formulate your rituals. Make them clear and precise. Eliminate wiggle room. Tie them to that burning vision emanating from the true you. The time for change is now. Put your rituals on paper, post or put them in areas where you will regularly see them, and begin your personal transformation.

THE PROGRESS-COMPASSION PARADIGM

Before you finalize and begin pursuing your first wave of rituals, there is one last concept we'd like to leave you with. We call it the Progress-Compassion Paradigm (Figure 15).

As we've discussed all along, this book is about transformation; it's about *making change*. Up until this point, we've spent a lot of time cultivating our self-awareness and doing the necessary things to set us up for the most meaningful and successful change possible. Now we are ready to implement that change. As we should, an intrinsic assumption we all have for that impending implementation is progress. We believe that we will set goals, pursue rituals, and achieve impactful changes in our lives. The great news is, not only will achieving our goals bring us greater happiness and performance, simply progressing toward them will as well. Carleton University Professor Timothy Pychyl reminds us of this point when he says, "To the extent that we're making progress on our goals, we're happier emotionally and more satisfied with our lives."[16] This point is something we're always eager to reinforce with the people we work with. Greater fulfillment starts at the first sign of progress. Keep moving forward and things will start to change. You will become happier.

As encouraging as it is to know that progress can be an immense source of satisfaction and fulfillment, it's important to acknowledge that, from time to time, progress is not possible. Sometimes we all fall down or fall short. We all have bad days. We all have tough weeks. In these moments, we urge you to be self-compassionate. We urge you to acknowledge the struggle that you're facing, be kind and open-hearted to yourself, and to realize that imperfection is part of the human experience. Couple forgiving yourself with pursuing progress and your change efforts will be more powerful. You will be growth-oriented without berating

PROGRESS   COMPASSION

FIGURE 15

or belittling yourself. With the Progress-Compassion Paradigm in mind, you will ultimately be successful.

Please, before proceeding to the next and final main section of this framework, take at least a little time to begin practicing your first rituals. Take enough time to start experiencing the beginnings of change in your life. If you do so, it will make the next section all the more powerful and relevant.

THE TOOLS
A SUMMARY

- **Change is often difficult because we don't anticipate our own psychology.** We have a very large logical/emotional divide within us that derails our change endeavors.

- When our change efforts fail, it's usually because our emotional center fatigues and conquers our logical desire for change. We represent this tug-of-war through Jonathan Haidt's metaphor of the logical Rider and the emotional Elephant.

- To achieve lasting change we must strive to form new habits by forming rituals that: (1) Roadmap the Rider and (2) Spur the Elephant so that they are moving in the same direction.

  ◆ Roadmap the Rider

    ▪ *Work We've Already Done*—All of the introspection and goal definition up until this point has created a great map.

    ▪ *Language*—Is your ritual clear? Does it tie to your change goal?

    ▪ *Write It Down*—Writing your rituals down increases your chance of achieving them by 40%.

  ◆ Spur the Elephant

    ▪ *Compelling Vision, Revisited*—Your ritual must **compel** you.

    ▪ *Support Group*—Lean on those you trust to help support you through the change process. Go to them when times are tough.

    ▪ *Face the Fear*—Find your inner courage to help you push through the fear you have around change.

◆ *Anticipate the Journey*

- Visualization—Visualize yourself throughout your ritual journey. Anticipate and plan for difficult moments.

- Energy Management—Space your rituals throughout the day. Don't attempt to implement them all at once.

- Action Triggers—Think about ways you can modify your environment to trigger and support your new behavior.

◆ *A Sense of Urgency*—Perhaps no other factor is as important to successful change as having a sense of urgency. The time for change is NOW.

● Progress-Compassion Paradigm: We are happier when we make progress on our goals. However, we are also human and we will have setbacks every once in a while. In those moments, treat yourself with compassion and pick yourself back up.

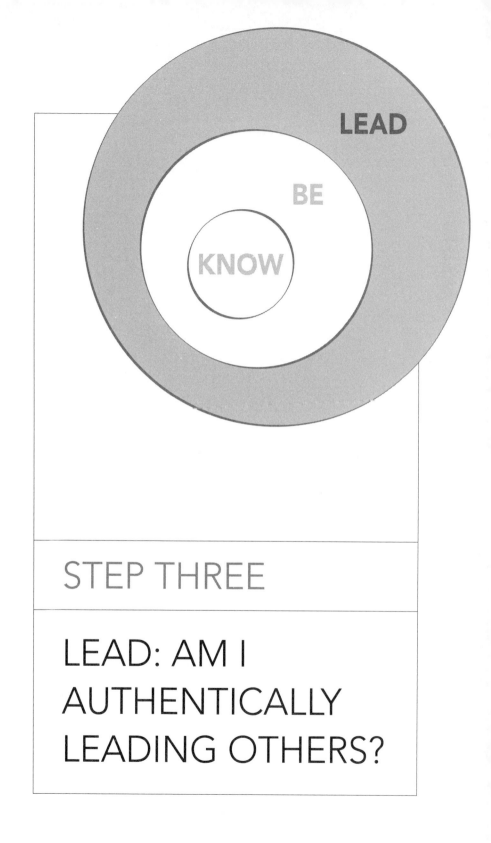

LEAD

BE

KNOW

STEP THREE

LEAD: AM I AUTHENTICALLY LEADING OTHERS?

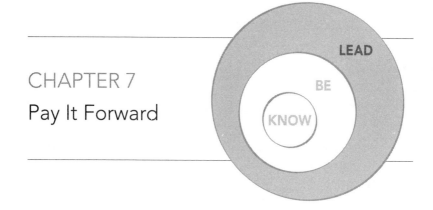

CHAPTER 7

Pay It Forward

As we discussed throughout KNOW-BE-LEAD, though we don't always realize it, we are all leaders. Each and every one of us is the leader of our own life. As such, we are directly responsible for the actions we take, the direction we pursue, and how we spend our time on a daily basis. Over the majority of this book, we have spent time dissecting this aspect of our leadership. We have spent time digging to the core of who we are and what gives us purpose, and we have written down our C-V Statement and reoriented our life in that direction. We, perhaps for the first time, are beginning to lead our lives in the direction of sustained fulfillment and alignment.

However, beyond simply leading ourselves, the vast majority of us LEAD others as well. We are employees, managers, executives, volunteers, mentors, coaches, husbands, wives, siblings, students, friends, and parents. Whether or not our title makes it explicit, **we all have a sphere of influence**; we all have a platform for leadership. The incredible thing about having improved your self-awareness, identified your core values, built personal rituals, and begun living closer to your calling is that you are now better suited to positively and effectively lead those around you. As the former CEO of Medtronic and current professor of management at Harvard Business School Bill George says, "When you follow

> Becoming an authentic leader is not easy. First, you have to understand yourself, because the hardest person you will ever have to lead is yourself. Once you have an understanding of your authentic self, you will find that leading others is much easier."
>
> –Bill George

your internal compass, your leadership will be authentic, and people will naturally want to associate with you."[1] People appreciate honesty. They appreciate consistency. They appreciate authenticity. Witnessing a leader who is in her element, who is living her calling day in and day out, is a sight to behold. It's a sight that teammates, employees, and mentees respond to. As you've gone through the pages of this book, you have begun moving toward this greater alignment, this authenticity. Accordingly, your ability to lead, connect with, and inspire others is already improving. The best news is, as you continue to heighten your self-awareness and build new rituals, your capacity for leading and positively affecting others will only continue to rise. This leadership ability is the focus of the third and final part of our framework. It's time to better LEAD others. Allow us to show you how.

A FAMILIAR FRAMEWORK

Although more effectively leading others hasn't been the sole purpose of the work we've done so far, it is certainly a major result. You see, in learning how to find greater personal fulfillment and performance for yourself, you've also learned to do the same for others. Put simply, to authentically LEAD others you must KNOW yourself, KNOW others, and help others KNOW themselves, along with BE in alignment with your core values and calling, and help others BE in alignment with theirs. Look familiar? The same principles that have thus far guided you to your greater fulfillment and performance are the same that will guide those you lead to theirs. On paper, it's really that simple. In practice, as we all know, it can be much harder. Throughout this chapter, we'll break down some strategies and perspectives for becoming a more authentic, effective, and inspirational leader.

KNOWING OTHERS AND HELPING OTHERS KNOW THEMSELVES

Part of discovering your calling and undergoing your own personal transformation is a heightened sense of awareness of both yourself and others. Having embarked on greater understanding of the true you, you have broken through the numerous pitfalls that many people misidentify with on a daily basis. You have realized who you are not, you have identified and labeled the ego within, and you have come to understand both the fundamental and underlying aspects of your personality. In successfully doing so, you've not only made realizations about your own identity, but you can now apply your perspective and learnings to others—both to better KNOW them and to help them better KNOW themselves.

Explicitly

Much like our starting point for KNOW, an explicit and relatively straightforward place to start better knowing others is via personality diagnostics. Personality diagnostic tools, like the Enneagram and MBTI along with the Authentic Feedback processes we discussed earlier, enable you to tangibly engage in knowing those you lead. With personality diagnostics, you, together with your teammates or colleagues, can sit down and go through the KNOW process together. You gain insight into your team's core orientations and perspectives. You learn about your team's workplace motivators. And the learning is twofold. As you come to know and understand them better, they come to know and understand themselves better. As you take a concrete step toward stronger leadership, they take a first step toward personal transformation.

As for having a go-to personality diagnostic to better know those you lead, it's clear that there are many options. Over the course of our experience, we've encountered a wide degree of diagnostic preference amongst different leaders. Some like the Enneagram most because of its fluid, relational nature (with its wings, functional and dysfunctional directions, and general interconnectedness of types). Others elect to use authentic feedback processes most often because of those processes' experience-based and explicitly observational nature. Still others prefer commonly used techniques like Myers-Briggs or the DISC assessment. Whatever method you choose, using one of these diagnostics or something similar can be extremely useful for your ability to understand and, thus, more effectively lead your team.

Remember Gary Knepp, the small-medium business executive from the Northwest? By doing a personality diagnostic and authentic feedback process with his company, he and his fellow executives were able to delve into the core of their leadership frustrations and set a new course of conduct and expectations for one another going forward. Remember Behnam's Enneagram example? He was able to enlighten both a class of groupthink Polish leaders and his relationship with his daughter using the Enneagram. Your capabilities are no less than Gary's and Behnam's. You can do the same.

Beyond using personality diagnostics and feedback processes, come up with creative ways to get to know others through meaningful conversation. Make the rounds once a week with the members of your team to have genuine work/life check-ins. Go grab "fun lunch" with your direct reports once a month. As many well-known leaders have done over the years, do bimonthly "fireside chats" with different groups of your colleagues. Get creative! There are numerous ways to explicitly reach out to those in your sphere of influence and get to know them better. As you do, mutual understanding will increase, bonds will strengthen, and your ability to effectively lead will grow.

Intuitively

In addition to explicitly getting to KNOW others through personality diagnostics, feedback processes, and other creative means, you will start to better understand and therefore better lead others based on the intuition you've begun to cultivate surrounding our identity pitfalls. You've witnessed personally how you have sometimes mistaken yourself for your things, your looks, your story, or your status. But you've come to the realization that these things are not you. They neither define nor control you. With these lessons in hand, with this awareness, you can begin to understand others more clearly. As you grow in self-awareness, you will more adeptly lead others because you are now more adept at understanding them on an intuitive level.

For example, an employee who frequently obsesses about or digs his heels in over the way things "have always been" isn't necessarily an annoying change-resistant worry-wart (although that's certainly how he comes off on the surface), rather he's just particularly attached to the words his ego is whispering in his ear. He is holding onto a story about how things have been and should continue to be. Perhaps the idea of change unleashes paralyzing fear and uncertainty within him. Knowing what you now know about how we are not the voice in our heads and we are not our stories, you can hopefully see through his predicament and: (1) treat him from a position of understanding and empathy and (2) help give him courage and subtly help him work toward overcoming his misidentification.

Similarly, you can now see more clearly during moments when things like tension and animosity consume your team because so many of those moments are ego-driven. They start with employee A attacking employee B's idea or position. Then employee B fights back, insisting that he's "right." They then get into a heated back-and-forth in which they simultaneously try to convince and demean one other. Each employee has his own set of beliefs that informs his opinion—which is completely fine, natural, and in the context of brainstorming or ideating, useful. However, when they introduce negativity, it's a clear indicator that both employees have misidentified with their attachment to their opinions. They defend themselves and harshly attack one another because they both see someone who disagrees with their opinion as someone who disapproves of them as people. They sense the other person trying to put a chink in their egoic armor and therefore fight back fervently. Fortunately, given the introspective journey you've been on, you can now begin to see this interpersonal tension for what it is. It's not a situation of two people hating each other (though it might very well seem like it); it's a situation where two egos have squared off against one another, mutually refusing to back down. With your evolving KNOW perspective, you will be able to avoid passing judgment in these kinds of tough interpersonal situations. Despite your potential desire to join in the fray or take sides, you will be able to see through each employees' misidentification and be able to treat them with levelheaded calmness. Having come to better know yourself, you will not only be a more effective leader, you will, through your example and dialogue, help them come to know more about themselves.

Whether you use personality and team dynamic diagnostics or simply lean on your greater intuitive perceptiveness and organic conversation, you will better understand others as you continue to nurture your self-awareness and pursue your personal transformation. When you better understand them, you can more effectively interact with and lead them. Whether it's by more adeptly establishing ground rules for brainstorming sessions and team meetings, by becoming more calm and effective when conflict arises, by assigning work more adeptly based on how people function best, or something else, your leadership will improve. It will become more in-touch and more powerful. It will become more authentic. And as we've said, when you bring KNOW into your leadership, not only will you better understand others, but you will help others better understand themselves. When they begin to understand themselves, they take their first step toward their own transformation and sustainable fulfillment. They take their first step toward putting their fingers on the pulse of their calling, on the pulse of greater performance, passion, and productivity. Now, that's a powerful thing.

THE LINK TO EMOTIONAL INTELLIGENCE

The idea that your leadership improves as you begin applying KNOW to yourself and others goes beyond the realm of intuitive explanation—it has been showcased by leadership psychology research. Many of you, if you've had any significant exposure to business or management, have probably encountered the concept of emotional intelligence. For those who haven't (and as a quick refresher for those who have), emotional intelligence is a term popularized in the mid-1990s by psychologist Daniel Goleman that describes an individual's ability to sense, assess, and control their feelings as well as the feelings of others. The higher one's emotional intelligence, the more proficient they are at connecting

with others, navigating conflict, self-soothing, and generally recognizing the human element in most situations.

When Goleman looked at emotional intelligence in the context of leadership, he found that it was profoundly important. He
discovered, "Effective leaders are alike in one crucial way: they
have a high degree of emotional intelligence."[2] Traditional smarts
such as technical skill or analytical ability are, of course, important
depending on your given leadership situation, but Goleman finds
that emotional intelligence is the biggest differentiator of excep-
tional leaders. When he studied the difference between standout
and average leaders in senior leadership positions, he found that
"nearly 90% of the difference in their profiles was attributable to
emotional intelligence factors rather than cognitive abilities."[3]

So what does emotional intelligence look like? Well, according
to Goleman's research it consists of the following five elements:
self-awareness, self-regulation, motivation, empathy, and social
skill (see Figure 16).[4] Though we could go into an in-depth breakdown of how living inside-out helps you embody each element,
we'll keep it quick and straightforward.

(1) *Self-awareness.* The entire first third of this book is dedicated
to this. You've gone through and are continuing to revisit KNOW.
You are cultivating an extremely strong sense of who you are and
how you feel about different situations and aspects of your life.

(2) *Self-regulation.* An important part of that self-awareness
process, self-regulation is something you've gotten better at by
recognizing who you are not. As you continue to work, you'll only
get better at quelling the avalanche of thoughts, emotions, and
stories that threaten to overwhelm and hijack you when the going
gets rough. You'll be able to regulate and maintain perspective by
making the conscious choice to step away from your ego in the
moment.

(3) *Motivation.* Now that you are living from the inside-out, you are more passionately aligned than ever before. You have a compelling C-V Statement. You are heading in a direction that is meaningful and fulfilling for you. You are motivated for reasons that go beyond the superficial.

(4) *Empathy.* As we've just discussed, as you apply the lessons of KNOW to others, you automatically begin understanding and being more compassionate toward them. You've grappled with and continue to face your own pitfalls and you can see the tug-of-war within others. You can relate to and navigate others' emotions more effectively than ever before.

(5) *Social Skill.* In a related vein to empathy, your social skill has improved by knowing others and helping them come to know

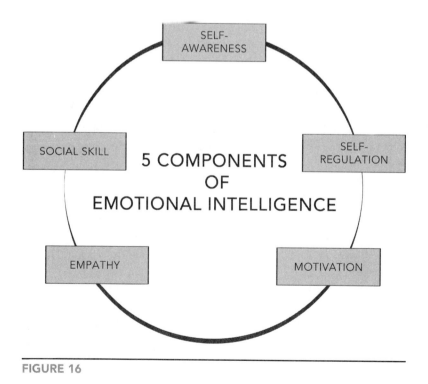

FIGURE 16

themselves. You've hopefully come to find others more relatable and, through helping them come to know themselves, are forging more meaningful, influential connections.

As you can see, by going through KNOW and BE, you are living the five components of emotional intelligence. You are cultivating a skill that is one of the strongest indicators of effective, transcendent leaders. Harness it and use it to positively affect others.

BE: LEARNING TO EMPOWER

Just as being in alignment was crucial for personal growth, it is also important for your effectiveness as a leader. When you lead in alignment with your core values, when you're true to your authentic self, people will want to follow you. They'll want to follow you because inner-outer alignment is a powerful sight. It radiates calm confidence. It radiates authenticity and honesty. It's simultaneously trustworthy and compelling. Beyond being in alignment with your own purpose and calling, you must also help those you lead be in alignment with theirs. When you do, you help bring them closer to their own meaning and fulfillment, as well as their own capacity for authentic leadership. When you help others BE, you empower them. You remind them that who they are and what they do matters. As we'll see shortly, that's one of the most powerful gifts you can give as a leader.

BE the Authentic You

Before you can help others be in alignment with their calling, you must consistently be in alignment with yours. Fortunately, the recipe for doing so can be found in the preceding chapters. As you go through the challenges of leading your team or organization, revisit the work you've done toward your own transformation. Continue pushing for greater self-awareness, keep identifying and labeling your ego when it pops up, revisit your C-V Statement and change goals, and methodically build new rituals. Your ability to live more in line with your authentic self is directly correlated to your ability to authentically lead those around you. Re-read and remember the notes, journal entries, and work you've done so far. They can all be useful reminders of the commitment you've made and the true self you want to become.

AUTHENTICITY AND INFLUENCE: THE LEADERSHIP NUANCE

Though living in personal alignment is an essential part of your enhanced ability to lead others, there's a bit more to the story. The reality is that not all aligned, authentic actions are created equal. Yes, many of the authentic things that you say to your colleagues or teammates have the ability to move and inspire them. However, some actions that you would consider authentic may have more of a neutral or, in some cases, negative effect on those you're trying to lead. Thus, there is another component of BEING an authentic leader worth noting: influence.

In order to truly unlock your capability as a leader, you must learn to harness the authentic parts of you that successfully influence others. When you do that, not only will you be living in personally fulfilling alignment but you'll also maximize your ability to affect others. You'll enter the realm of credible leadership (see Figure 17).

While the words "credible leader" might not necessarily be the most exhilarating descriptors of all time, research done by leadership scholars James Kouzes and Barry Posner shows that credibility is the quality that people most desire in their leaders.[6] In a ten-year study of thousands of middle and top-level managers, Kouzes and Posner found that three of the top four most important

"If you want to be trusted, be honest. If you want to be honest, be true. If you want to be true, be yourself."

–Anonymous

leadership characteristics were *honesty, competence, and the ability to inspire.* They cross-referenced these three traits with a standard sociological definition of credibility— "trustworthiness, expertise, and dynamism"—and saw a nearly perfect match. People want to follow credible people. Kouzes and Posner concluded, "Above all else, we must be able to believe in our leaders. We must believe they will do what they say and that they have the knowledge and skill to lead. They must be enthusiastic about the direction in which we are headed."[7]

Kouzes and Posner note that credibility is something that must be cultivated over time. It's earned as a result of continuous authentic and influential actions, and by a commitment to honesty, competence, and inspirational energy. In their research, they narrow in on five fundamental actions for cultivating credibility. These actions, listed below, are essential for authentic leadership.

1. Know Those You Lead

2. Stand Up for Your Beliefs

3. Communicate Passionately

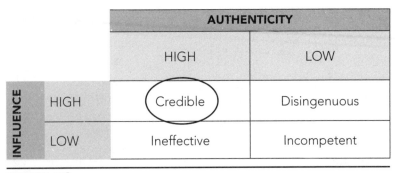

		AUTHENTICITY	
		HIGH	LOW
INFLUENCE	HIGH	Credible	Disingenuous
	LOW	Ineffective	Incompetent

FIGURE 17[5]

4. Lead by Example

5. Conquer Yourself

1. Know Those You Lead

There's not much to say here that hasn't already been said. Knowing others is an essential part of our authentic leadership framework and is something that, through the work you've done in this book, you already have a huge leg-up on.

2. Stand Up for Your Beliefs

This is all about alignment and authenticity. Credible leaders have the courage to stand in line with their vision and core values even when it's difficult. Doing so builds trust and a sense of honesty with your followers.

3. Communicate Passionately

This is an extremely important part of building authentic, credible leadership. After you've gone through KNOW and BE and have a true sense of *who you are*, the way you share that with the world is in the way you communicate. So communicate passionately! Share your purpose with energy. Talk about your team's vision like it matters (because it does). If you're leading authentically, every conversation you have and every endeavor you take on should tie back to the vision you've committed to. If it doesn't, you need to ask yourself why you're having that conversation. When you communicate passionately, you move, touch, and inspire others. You make sure that they not only see the vision, but that they breathe it as well. You're charismatic. Passionate communication breeds a leadership ripple effect: Your words become their words and your entire team or organization commits to the vision that has been laid out. More than anything, as you strive to cultivate your leadership through passionate communication, remember that your word must become your world. The things you say and write must be followed through on and, for the sake of your fulfillment and performance, should be in line with the calling you're trying to live out.

4. Lead by Example

One of the best ways to tangibly demonstrate inner-outer alignment as a leader is to lead by example. Whatever your and your organization's or team's or family's core values are, live them day-to-day. Share your growth mindset with others by encouraging risk-taking and learning from failure (it's all too easy to penalize in those situations—watch out for that trap!). Like a good coach, model and teach your values through your behavior. Strive for that alignment.

5. Conquer Yourself

Credibility is built when you have a calm confidence in who you are and where you are going. When you have a strong sense of the true you and have faced and dealt with your identity pitfalls and fears surrounding change, you inspire the confidence of others. They look to you to lead.

As you can see, though the core of your greater leadership effectiveness is based in your newfound alignment and authenticity, the details are a little more nuanced. Seek to take authentic action that is also influential, as well as remember the actions recommended by Kouzes and Posner and you will build your credibility. You will solidify your position as someone who inspires and leads others.

WHY NOT KNOW-BE-MANAGE?

One of the questions we are often asked when discussing authentic leadership is: How does *managing* others fit in? It's important to note that the assumption underlying the question is that there is a difference between leading and managing. On one level, we agree with that assumption. We're fond of the Warren Bennis quote that illustrates their difference yet mutual importance: "Managers are people who do things right and leaders are people who do the right things." However, leading and managing are really more connected than some would have you believe. To illustrate this point, allow us to introduce a case Behnam teaches to many of our clients about two businessmen, Renn and Fred.

MEET RENN[8]

Renn Zaphiropoulos is the president of Versatec, Inc., the world's largest producer of electrostatic printers and plotters. As the leader of the company, he sees himself as the one responsible for motivating his employees to do work that is in line with the overall plan; however, he doesn't believe in ordering anyone to do anything. He describes his job as needing to find the grain of the situation and then go with it, not against it—much like sailing. He adjusts the sails and subtly steers along with way.

Renn doesn't make big product or market decisions. He instead creates the right conditions under which those decisions can be made. To do so, he believes in frequent, friendly contact with people to see how they are doing and how he can better help them excel. Renn says he's very sensitive to stupid policies and, therefore, he tries not to have a lot of rules. He's not too concerned with formality—suits are a rarity for him and his employees. For Renn, effort is not key, results are.

Described by his employees as the "company psychiatrist," "employee advocate," "eternal optimist," and "long-term visionary," Renn is a skilled leader who knows how to motivate and bring out the best in his employees. He is very personable and his employees trust him. With the exception of a couple of instances where a few employees wished he would have been tougher, Renn is lauded as a great leader who always gets the company the results it needs.

MEET FRED[9]

Fred Henderson is the Western Region's general manager for Xerox's Information Systems Group (ISG), USA. ISG's five regional general managers are responsible for almost 20 yearly sales, service, budgetary control, affirmative action, and profit goals. Fred's Western Region has outperformed all of the other regions for the last three years and is leading again this year.

Fred sees himself as in charge of creating an environment and atmosphere that provides the people in his region with the opportunity to achieve their goals and enjoy their work, while maintaining a strict attention to detail and step-by-step progress. To do this, he has a very precise management cycle associated with establishing priorities, committing to specific objectives, reviewing performance, and forming corrective action plans when necessary. Fred believes decision-making should be hands-on, decisive, and reflective of good judgment. Effective delegation is one of his ongoing objectives.

Fred is a very precise and detail-oriented man. He also believes strongly in a purposeful approach to career guidance as he spends a lot of time with people discussing people-related issues. Described by his employees as "strong-willed," "fair and honest," "straightforward," and "competitive, tenacious, and tough-minded," Fred is a very successful guy who keeps his people moving and besting their competition year after year.

Any time Behnam teaches this case, he asks the participants to indicate, by a show of hands, which man they'd prefer to work for. Without fail, at least ¾ of the room says Renn. After pausing for a moment to let the number of raised hands sink in, he quickly turns the question around and asks which man they'd prefer to have work for them. The inverse happens. All of a sudden, over ¾ of the hands go up for Fred.

This flip-flop is fairly easy to anticipate. On the traditional managing-leading continuum, Fred comes out more on the managing side due to all of his attention to detail and hands-on approach. He seems like a responsible, get-things-done-and-then-some type of guy who most people would love to employ or lead. Renn, on the other hand, is situated more on the leading side of things. He is more of a big-picture visionary who doesn't meddle too much in people's day-to-day autonomy. The freedom and trust he provides his employees is appealing to the majority of people, and thus he's the more popular boss selection. This difference has significant implications for the realities of everyday leadership. Just think. If, when you're in a position of leadership, you're most fond of the Freds who are working for you, you will eventually reward and promote them. Over time, these promoted Freds will become the next wave of organizational leaders. Though they're efficient and get the job done, the majority of the people working under them would have preferred Renn. So, you see, there's a bit of a dilemma from a pragmatic leadership standpoint. The dilemma reveals the telling link between managing and leading and that's that, as a truly effective leader, you have to do both. You must be both the leader and the manager. You can be the visionary, but you still have to be aware of and ready to act on the details. As Jim March, a well-known professor emeritus at the Stanford Business School, always said, "Leadership is not just about having vision; it's also about making sure the bathrooms are clean." Remember that though you are LEADING, an important part of that duty is knowing how and when to get tactical. The best leaders also know how to, when necessary, manage others. Don't forget about your toilet scrubber when the moment calls for it.

HELPING OTHERS BE

Beyond the nuances of how to BE in influential alignment as an authentic leader, you must also think about how to empower those around you. Just as you help them KNOW, you must also help them BE. You must help them BE in alignment with their core values and their calling. You must help them create meaning, fulfillment, and greater performance in their lives.

The primary way to help others BE is to take action based upon how you come to KNOW them. What makes them tick? What is their Enneagram? Which values do they hold closest? How do they process new information? What about their work motivates them? Which times during the day do they seem most productive? Knowing the answers to these kinds of questions is perhaps the strongest step toward helping them BE. When you know these answers, you can delegate work, assign projects, and motivate optimally. You can maximize both your team's performance and the meaning they derive from their work. By beginning to understand the nature of your followers' callings, you can begin injecting more meaning and fulfillment into their work. People will produce more and be happier simultaneously.

Obviously, this personal level of knowing and subsequent empowerment is only feasible on a limited scale. As a CEO of a 600-person company, there is no way that you can do this on an individual level for each one of your employees. However, it is entirely feasible in a trickle-down scenario. If you are the CEO, make it your job to help your VPs BE in greater alignment. Instruct them to do the same for their senior managers. The senior managers for the middle level managers. The middle managers for the project leads. The project leads for the project team members. And the project team members for the team interns. If everyone makes it their duty to help those in their sphere of influence BE in greater alignment, you will have more effective, authentic, and productive leaders at every level of your organization.

THE PYGMALION EFFECT

Beyond empowering others by helping them live in greater personal alignment, you can also bring out the best in them by changing your fundamental view toward them. Though it may sound overly simple, it turns out that people respond very strongly to the beliefs and expectations their leaders have of them. It's a phenomenon that has come to be called the Pygmalion Effect.

Named after an ancient fictional sculptor who fell in love with a statue of a woman he had carved after it came to life, the Pygmalion Effect was formally discovered and researched in the 1960s by Harvard psychologist Robert Rosenthal and elementary school principal Lenore Jacobson.[10] Rosenthal was, at the time, researching self-fulfilling prophecies and posited that teachers' fundamental view of their students would affect their students' performance and behavior. In collaboration with Jacobson, Rosenthal studied and was able to confirm this hypothesis. When the teachers they studied were given randomized information that certain students had higher IQs than others, the teachers subconsciously behaved in ways that facilitated the high-IQ students' success. The teachers *believed* something about a certain group of students. Accordingly, the teachers *acted* a specific way toward those students and subsequently, those students *performed* to a higher level than their peers (see Figure 18). The power of the teachers' beliefs and expectations was undeniable.

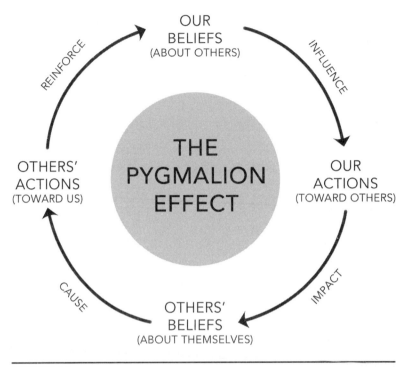

FIGURE 18

In the decades following the Rosenthal-Jacobson study, the power of the Pygmalion Effect has been shown time and time again. It has been showcased in athletics, in business, in education, and in individual families. In management, it has garnered a lot of attention as a defining characteristic of effective leadership. Leaders who believe that their followers are highly capable treat and motivate them as such. The result, more often than not, is that their followers live up to the standard and perform at a high level. The opposite, of course, is also true. Leaders who see and treat their followers as incapable and inadequate often end up with team members or employees who underperform and disappoint.

The fortunate thing about leading authentically is that you naturally assume a positive Pygmalion role. You are able to let go of your and others' egoic attachments and see most situations without clinging to a negative story. You see opportunity and humanity in the large majority of your interactions and therefore treat those you lead with compassion and understanding. You treat people

> "The task of leadership is not to put greatness into humanity, but to elicit it, for the greatness is already there."
>
> –John Buchan

capably and assure them of their ability even when times are tough. Because you want to help others BE, you should lead with the expectation that people are worthy of meaningful, intrinsically motivating work. When you do so, the people that you lead will come to believe it and will push themselves to find it. As they do over time, they'll move toward greater fulfillment and performance.

About the Authors: Behnam's First Pygmalion Experience

When I was a PhD student, I was a process facilitator for an MBA course on interpersonal dynamics. After one week of successful facilitation among several groups in the course, the professor told me about this challenging student in a group I hadn't yet worked with. The student, he said, had been in the Israeli army and was incredibly tough and confrontational. He paired me with this guy's group and wished me good luck!

So over I went, attempting to muster up the courage to work with this confident, in-your-face former soldier. As I sat down with his group, there he was. Big, athletic, strident. I could feel myself starting to judge and vilify him; however, before I got too far down that path, my determination to get through to him came roaring to the surface. You know, I thought to myself, this guy is just like my jock brother, Hormoz. I love this guy. I can talk to him, no problem.

Over the course of our 45-minute session, I gave him feedback with the same care and genuineness as I would have given my brother. I saw him not as a rough and tough instigator but as someone capable of connection and meaningful relationships.

At the end of our session, as was the custom for the class, the students in each group gave feedback to that day's facilitator. When it came to the soldier's turn to speak in our group, he told me that I had been the most effective and connected facilitator he had yet had, and he thanked me for the effort I had made. Wow, what a moment! By simply humanizing this guy, by seeing beyond his rough exterior, I was able to draw out his humanity and kindness. It's a leadership lesson that has stuck with me to this day. Eliminate negative assumptions and judgments about others and go in with a high bar and people will continually rise to the occasion; they will continuously surprise you.

It's worth noting that the Pygmalion Effect doesn't just apply to how you view others—it also applies to how you view yourself. Closely linked to having a growth mindset (which, remember, is one of our biggest overarching asks of you throughout this process), applying the Pygmalion Effect to your life is all about the fundamental view you choose to have of yourself. See yourself as someone worthy of fulfillment, as someone who is resilient in the face of setbacks, and as someone who is always thirsting to learn and grow, and it will be so. You have that power. You set that tone. As you live your calling, you can see the Pygmalion Effect play out in your own life as well as the lives of those you lead.

ENGAGE OTHERS

Outside of empowering those you lead in an individually tailored way or through the Pygmalion Effect, you can help them

find more mean-
ing in their work
by committing to
engage them. Accord-
ing to William Kahn,
an organizational be-
havior professor at the

> " Whether you think you can, or you think you can't—you're right."
>
> –Henry Ford

Boston University School of Management, engagement is "the
state in which individuals express their entire self—physically,
cognitively, and emotionally—in their role."[11] In other words, it's
when they experience significant degrees of alignment with what
they do.

One way to meaningfully engage those you lead is through a
process described by Harvard organizational psychologist Rich-
ard Hackman.[12] As a result of his research, he says that there are
three straightforward yet powerful conditions for employees to be
more engaged and fulfilled in the work that they do. Number one,
they should have to use multiple faculties and abilities to complete the work. In other words, the task should not be assembly-
line-esque. Second, they should complete the whole project—or
at least a meaningful part of it—from beginning to end. They
should feel like they made a measurable contribution. Lastly, they
should have a sense that their work has made an impact on other
people—either their colleagues or customers. These three things
are easy to do and can make a huge difference in how the people
you lead feel about their work.

As Hackman's three-point strategy alludes to, people are engaged and find their work fulfilling when they feel like they've had
a *meaningful* hand in a *meaningful* task. There is perhaps no bigger or better place for them to do this than with team, company,
or organizational goal and vision-setting. All too often, we see
leaders—from executives to middle managers—unveil a complete

vision roadmap in an entirely top-down fashion as if to say, "Here we go people. This is the plan. We're sticking to it. Now buy in." However, what these leaders often forget is that people support what they help create. By being completely top-down in the fundamental mission of the organization, product, or project, leaders miss out on an immense opportunity to collect input and buy-in from those they lead. We often say, "If they're involved in making the baby, they'll help take care of the baby." Give those you lead an opportunity to be the authors of change. Of course, this doesn't mean that every organizational goal or strategy should go to a democratic vote. As we mentioned earlier, crafting a clear and compelling North Star is one of the most important responsibilities of leaders at the top of their organizations. However, as a technique for empowering others, gathering and then acknowledging input on major decisions is extremely effective. We always recommend that leaders nurture an environment where people are not only welcome to give input but are emphatically encouraged and incentivized to do so. When people feel like they are being heard, particularly on big-picture objectives, they feel like they matter in a big way. Give them that context. Create those avenues of communication. Encourage, reward, and then acknowledge those who contribute to charting the course for your organization. It will engage and create yet another layer of meaning for those you lead.

But Really . . .

Make sure you *actually* make the constant effort to engage those you lead in meaningful work. Probably, no matter how much you think you do it or can do it, you can always do more. Research has shown that leaders significantly overestimate how much they engage their employees (see Figure 19). Try to avoid this discrepancy by making meaningful engagement a core part of how you help others BE.

Does your leader do the following very often?	% of Leaders Who Feel Like They Do	% of Followers Who Feel Like Their Leaders Do
Give More Responsibility	48%	10%
Give Sincere Praise	80%	14%
Give More Interesting Work	51%	5%

FIGURE 19[13]

SERVICE LEADERSHIP

Jack Welch once said, "The day you become a leader, it becomes about them. Your job is to walk around with a can of water in one hand and a can of fertilizer in the other hand. Think of your team as seeds and try to build a garden. It's about building these people."[14] His words touch on what we believe is one of the most fundamental tenants of effective leadership: Leadership is about serving those around you.

When you approach leadership with a service mindset there are multiple benefits. On one hand, you continuously empower and inspire those you lead. You see, serving others implies sacrifice. It means working hard and making yourself available for others. Servant leaders lead by example and are constantly involved in supporting the members of their team. Second, servant leadership helps ensure that people are leading authentically. When you're most concerned with doing what's best for the group rather than yourself, it makes it difficult for your ego to get in the way of the true you. In that sense, servant leadership keeps you grounded. Thirdly, leading with a service mindset makes you powerful rather than forceful. What we mean by that is, rather than being manipulative and coercive, servant leaders are dynamic, confidence-inspiring, and focused on setting others up to succeed. They powerfully build collective passion through their energy and optimism, rather than build resentment by imposing their will on others. Fourth and finally, leading by serving others has tremendous implications for the level of personal meaning and happiness you derive from what you do. In the words of Ralph Waldo Emerson, "It is one of the most beautiful compensations of this life that no man can sincerely try to help another without helping himself." Pursuing servant leadership brings you happiness; it brings you closer to personal meaning. Serving others simultaneously inspires, keeps you humble, and benefits you in the deepest and most important ways. Don't forget it.

LEADING AUTHENTICALLY AT HOME

Though most of our discussion throughout this section has centered on authentic leadership in the context of organizations and teams, it is certainly not confined to the professional realm. Nearly everything we've mentioned in LEAD can also be applied in your personal life. To be a better spouse, take the time to truly KNOW your partner on an ego-less level. BE in alignment with your true self and help your spouse BE in alignment with theirs. Same goes for your children. Think about how to nurture their sense of self. Teach them that learning how to breathe (hey, maybe even mini-meditate!), smile, and express gratitude is just as important as learning their multiplication tables. Leading your family authentically will help bring out the best in them. You'll have more patience, they'll feel more loved, and in time you'll grow into a more self-aware household.

Time to LEAD

We hope that the preceding pages have showcased how the work you've done in KNOW and BE has brought you into the realm of authentic leadership. Leading others is never an easy or straightforward task. However, with the lessons you've learned throughout your personal transformation process, you are now more equipped to effectively inspire, lead, and transform those around you. As you continue to become more connected and aligned with your true self, you will continue to become a more authentic leader. Over time, as your friends, family, colleagues, and teammates interact with you, they will be able to sense your ever-increasing alignment,

> " The most dangerous leadership myth is that leaders are born—that there is a genetic factor to leadership. This myth asserts that people simply either have certain charismatic qualities or not. That's nonsense. In fact, the opposite is true. Leaders are made rather than born."
>
> *–Warren Bennis*

your personal purpose, and your passion. As you master the art of transcending your ego and living in the present moment, your ability to genuinely connect to others will skyrocket. As you engage people in meaningful work, their loyalty will grow. And as you truly embody a service leadership mindset, your ability to inspire will flourish. All the work you've done and will hopefully continue to do in KNOW and BE has enabled you to take your leadership to the next level. As you've begun to better LEAD yourself, you can now better LEAD others.

Gandhi: A Man Who Had to Lead Himself Before Leading Others

Mohandas Gandhi, the man who would eventually become the "Father of India" and known throughout the world as Mahatma (meaning "Great Soul") Gandhi, did not begin his life in a way many would expect.

As a child and young adult, Gandhi was quite opposite the man who would come to be known as a worldwide symbol of peace, nonviolent civil disobedience, and persistence. Born in Porbandar, India, Gandhi was extremely shy and fearful as a boy. He describes, "I used to be very shy and avoided all company. . . . To be at school at the stroke of the hour and to run back home as soon as the school closed—that was my daily habit. I literally ran back, because I could not bear to talk to anybody. I was even afraid lest anyone should poke fun at me."[15] Gandhi's fear extended beyond the judgment and teasing of others and into the realm of snakes, ghosts, and murderers. He feared the dark for that's when he imagined the ghouls and serpents would come for him.

When Gandhi was thirteen, he was, per his cultural tradition, arranged and married to a fourteen-year-old girl named Kasturbai. Attractive and patient, Kasturbai slowly became the object of Gandhi's affection (again, he was still incredibly shy). As Gandhi grew comfortable with her, he became a demanding and envious husband. He thought about her all the time and hated being away from her. Even though Gandhi married and finished high school, he still was a young man consumed by fear. He noted how he was unable to share his fears with his wife because he felt ashamed. She wasn't afraid of the dark or the ghouls of the night, so he quietly kept his nervousness to himself.

Alongside Gandhi's fear and shyness as a young man, he also struggled academically. He remembers having a very difficult time learning his multiplication tables as a boy and, even throughout high school, was a mediocre student. After high school, he enrolled in college thinking he might try to become a doctor. However, those notions were short-lived because, within five months, he was failing all of his classes and withdrew from school. Gandhi was directionless and disillusioned. On a whim, Gandhi's uncle recommended that he go to London to study law. After all, the

British were the imperial rulers of India and, thus, a British degree would probably assure some level of success. Despite worries about missing his home and family, Gandhi gathered up the courage and the funds and decided to go.

In the beginning, Gandhi's London experience was extremely difficult. Both on the voyage and during his first months in London, he was incredibly lonely. Surrounded by a strange language and culture, Gandhi felt out of place everywhere he went. He was overwhelmingly sad, and cried himself to sleep on a regular basis. To quell his sadness, Gandhi decided to try to learn the ways of the English. He decided to try to become an English gentleman. He bought fancy suits and silk top hats, learned to tie a tie, and hired instructors to teach him the violin, the foxtrot, and to improve his English. However, Gandhi soon realized that his imitation lifestyle only made him more insecure. As famed Gandhi biographer Eknath Easwaran wrote, "The gap that he [Gandhi] sensed between his inner and outer selves was widening into a chasm."[16]

In response to the inner disconnect he felt about trying to pursue the gentleman lifestyle, Gandhi embarked on a mission to try to be truer to himself. He attempted to pursue a simpler life for the remainder of his time in London—he gave up all the lessons and propriety, moved into a one-room studio, walked everywhere he went, and further committed to and explored his culture's vegetarian diet. Unlike the academic turbulence he experienced back home, Gandhi found most of Britain's legal examinations straightforward and passed easily after three years. Upon his completion, he sailed home.

Unfortunately for Gandhi, his degree did not translate into courtroom proficiency. Having studied in Britain, he did not have a good understanding of the Indian court system. He failed utterly in several early attempts to apply Indian law to real-world scenarios. Even more detrimental, Gandhi had no confidence—he was still a man consumed by fear. In his first (and as it turns out, last) case in Bombay, Gandhi froze when trying to cross-examine a witness. Unable to find the words, he handed the case to another lawyer and left the courtroom in disgrace, laughter ringing out behind him.

Just as it seemed that he was tumbling down into a new low, an opportunity arose that Gandhi would later describe as an *act of grace*—he was offered a one-year clerical position at a local Muslim firm's South African office. When he arrived in South Africa, he immediately realized that there had been some kind of miscommunication in his job description. What he anticipated to be a one-year, paper-pushing clerical job was actually a detailed accounting role on a case with years of complicated and poorly recorded transaction records. He was supposed to decipher the mess and advise the company's legal counsel. Gandhi's first reaction, realizing that he was even less competent as an accountant than he had thus far been as a lawyer, was that, once again, he had set himself up for failure. However, it was at that moment that he recognized a pattern that had been building in his life. Every time setbacks occurred or failure threatened, he had run away. And where had it gotten him? He realized that his "run away and try to change my circumstances" approach had just brought him face-to-face with new failures. Therefore, this time Gandhi decided to do something different. He decided, rather than changing his circumstances, he would change himself. As Easwaran says, "Battered by failure, with nowhere left to look for help outside, he was ready to turn inward on his long journey of self-discovery."[17]

Gandhi threw himself into the case. He studied accounting and immersed himself in all the case's facts and nuances. Beyond any sort of lawyering, he was most interested in uncovering truth. He set himself to that task. Eventually, Gandhi knew both sides of the case better than anyone else, and, because he saw the case as a whole, he realized that it would probably be drawn out for months in the courts. Seeing that as an unsatisfactory outcome for both parties, Gandhi was able to slowly convince both sides, their lawyers included, to settle out of court. It was a huge breakthrough for Gandhi. He, for the first time, saw his work as service. He learned how to connect with people in a deep and meaningful way.

In the coming months and years, Gandhi's reputation in his South African community grew. Within a short time, his penchant for service and honesty made him very popular. For a while, his success translated into the material wealth commonly associated with a successful lawyer. He valued his professionalism and, upon moving his family to South Africa, insisted that they adopt the clothes and customs of their new culture. However, after a while, as he continued to witness and work against the abuses suffered by minorities in South Africa, he began to care less and less about the material things in his life. He saw that his things frequently got in the way of his service and thus resolved to simplify his life. As he simplified, he saw that he was able to unlock the full range of his energy, intellect, and effectiveness—moreover, though it was difficult to give up his material wealth at first, he began to experience unparalleled personal happiness. As his breakthrough began to crystallize, Gandhi wrote about he who lives a life of service: "He will be calm, free from anger and unruffled in mind even if he finds himself inconvenienced. His service, like virtue, is its own reward, and he will rest content with it."[18]

Gandhi continued to simplify his life—he gave up his unnecessary furniture, learned to cut his own hair, and began cleaning his own outhouse. Simultaneously, he began serving those around him more and more. He became a volunteer nurse, started an Indian news magazine, and formed an Indian ambulance corps. In the time that followed, as he wrote about Indian South African issues and tended to bloody, sometimes-massacred bodies. He continued

> "Consciously or unconsciously, every one of us does render some service or other. If we cultivate the habit of doing this service deliberately, our desire for service will steadily grow stronger, and will make not only for our own happiness but that of the world at large."
>
> –Gandhi

to search for the art of living and the true way. He prayed, meditated, and introspected on how he could best help himself help others. Eventually, he discovered the wisdom in the Bhagavad Gita (which he would come to call his "spiritual reference book"), became aware of the core aspects of who he was, and made some fundamental realizations about the human condition, which Easwaran wrote, "released all the love within him into his conscious control. He had begun to transform the last of his passions into spiritual power."[19]

As many of us know, Gandhi would go on to lead successful minority movements in both South Africa and India. He was a champion of civil rights, equality, and freedom. He became the global face of civil disobedience, a freedom fighter who never lifted a weapon. Gandhi began life as a fearful, uncertain man, who was a jealous and controlling husband, but who, over the course of his experience, came to believe in the power of love and saw service as the means to personal and collective well-being. In the end, he was the face of a nation. He was the symbol of Indian freedom from British rule, and he endures as a worldwide symbol of peace and human dignity today. His journey is a testimony to how overcoming fear and serving others can catalyze personal transformation and unlock one's full potential and personal fulfillment.

THE TOOLS
A SUMMARY

- This chapter is all about how the work you've done throughout the book has brought you to the doorstep of leading others effectively and authentically. Here's how it breaks down:

- KNOWING Others and Helping Them KNOW Themselves

  ◆ Explicitly—Use personality diagnostics, authentic feedback processes, or tools of your own creation to explicitly get to know others and help them better know themselves.

  ◆ Intuitively—The self-awareness you've cultivated throughout your personal transformation has put you at a huge advantage for seeing past others' pitfalls and treating them with calm understanding and empathy.

  ◆ After going through KNOW and BE, you've heightened your emotional intelligence, which is a distinguishing trait of highly effective leaders.

- BEING in Personal Alignment

  ◆ Beyond being authentic to who you are, you must also consider which parts of your authenticity are influential. When you do so, you find your zone of credible leadership.

    ■ Credibility is the trait that followers most value in their leaders.

    ■ It can be built by knowing those you lead, standing up for your beliefs, communicating passionately, leading by example, and conquering yourself. All of which are natural when leading authentically from the inside-out.

- ◆ Why not KNOW-BE-MANAGE?
  - ▪ BEING an effective leader means realizing that you must be able to both lead and manage. It's not an either-or scenario.
- ● Helping Others BE
  - ◆ As you come to KNOW others, helping them BE is really about creating opportunities for them to live and work in alignment.
  - ◆ Use the Pygmalion Effect—People generally act in line with what's expected of them. Model fulfillment and encourage them to take on projects that are meaningful and important. They'll do it and be glad they did.
  - ◆ Engage Others—People support what they help create. They value being involved in sufficiently challenging, complete tasks that make a difference to either their colleagues or their customers.
    - ▪ Leaders often overestimate how much they engage their followers. Ensure you don't make that mistake by making follower-engagement an essential part of how you LEAD.
- ● Service Leadership
  - ◆ Don't lose sight of the fact that leadership is service to others. If you're just doing it for the "glory" and the "power," you're doing it for the wrong reasons—you're just feeding your ego. Remember: "No man can sincerely try to help another without helping himself." It's a win-win.

NATE'S STATUS UPDATE

As we mentioned at the end of Chapter 6, Nate's first transformation ritual was to come home by 6 pm on Mondays, Wednesdays, and Fridays so that he could pursue his change goal of spending more quality time with his family. His second ritual was based on his change goal to become healthier and more physically fit:

Nate—RITUAL 2

Ritual: *Jog from 11:30 am–Noon on Tuesdays and Thursdays. Jog 45–60 minutes on Saturday mornings with Izzie.*

Target Goal: *Lose 15 lbs. Gain more energy.*

Why It Matters/Tie to Vision: *I know that to truly do best by others, I must do best by myself. I am committed to my health—both for my own sake, but also for my wife, my children, and my one-day grandchildren. I want to be alive and healthy for as many graduations, weddings, and precious moments as I can. My C-V Statement reads: "I will make exercise and healthy habits a priority, even if they appear inconvenient." I am committed to these words.*

Anticipating the Journey: *Set up calendar reminders for the jogging days at work. Also, ask Antoine (one of my colleagues) if he'd be interested in joining me from time to time. Keep running shoes, workout clothes, and clean underwear, along with soap and a towel, in a gym bag in my office.*

Start Date: *Next week (April 14).*

Pull My Elephant: *Heart disease is the leading cause of death in the United States, accounting for over ¼ of* *annual deaths. The leading risk factors are* **inactivity** *and* **obesity**. *Since I am committed to my future, I will fight to stay active and at a healthy weight. When a run seems inconvenient, remember: I want to grow old with Chloe and hold my grandchildren. I want to walk my daughter, Amy, down the aisle someday.*

After only a few days of his new rituals, Nate's colleagues and teammates began to notice a change. As he was packing up around 5:30 pm on the Wednesday of that first week, Dean, another director, poked his head into Nate's office and remarked with surprise at him leaving early. Nate explained how he was trying to get more evening time with Chloe and the kids and that he had already managed to power through that day's work in order to do so. Dean's face filled with amazement and disbelief. "Good for you, man. Good for you," he said as he gave Nate's doorframe a few pats and continued on down the hall. Similarly, as Nate walked past his boss Maria's office clad in running shoes and gym shorts on week one's Thursday morning, she couldn't help but call out incredulously, "What the hell are you doing?!" After a quick explanation, Nate headed out the door to the sound of his boss's congratulatory applause.

Three weeks into his new rituals, not only has Nate's new behavior caught the eye of most of his colleagues, it seems to have helped catalyze a change in his effectiveness with them as well. Several of the people on his team have expressed open appreciation for his lead-by-example reminder of the importance of work/life balance. One of them, Leah, even asked to join him and Antoine on their Tuesday/Thursday runs. When working with his team, Nate has noticed that he has begun to feel a little lighter. He has felt more focused and on point. He has brought more energy to group meetings and is becoming quicker at picking up on and dealing with conflict. In fact, just two weeks into his new rituals, he decided to tell his team about his third change goal: He wants to increase the team's sense of cohesion and positivity. Though he hasn't yet brought things like PQ Reps and the Enneagram to their attention (he plans to do so soon by forming a new ritual), his comments and the effects of his first two rituals are starting to change the team's dynamic. He has started treating his team with more compassion and understanding. He is really trying to KNOW and connect with them. As he's done so, members of his team have followed suit. They've picked each other up and shown up for one another in a way they haven't recently. Though it's just in the beginning stages, Nate has begun to feel the Pygmalion Effect take root—the tone and goal he has set is beginning to be mirrored in the actions of those he leads.

Through both the initial work Nate has done with his rituals and his ongoing journey toward greater self-knowing through his gratitude journal and his PQ Reps, Nate has begun to sense a shift in his life. Though it's certainly not a night-and-day difference, things are beginning to change. And it's not just at work. At home, Chloe has been blown away by his Saturday morning runs with Izzie. His engaged and energetic presence three times a week for dinner has left her even more stunned. Although it's not as if every struggle they've been having has disappeared, he and Chloe do find themselves smiling more often than before. A simple appreciation and graciousness has begun creeping back into their relationship over the last three weeks, and they both are loving it. For the first time in a while, Nate feels like he and Chloe are finding common ground with one another.

In just three weeks, Nate is finding more energy and meaning in the work he's doing. He's feeling more connected to his wife and children than he has in a long time. And he's feeling like, for the first time in the last year-and-a-half, he's growing closer to happiness, fulfillment, and his peak performance. Though it's a long, continuous process ahead, he's thrilled to see where it goes.

THE ROAD AHEAD

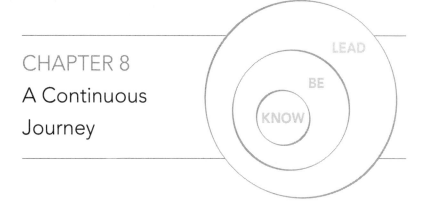

CHAPTER 8

A Continuous Journey

Though we've taken our first pass through KNOW-BE-LEAD, living your calling does not stop here. It must actually be *lived*. Doing so goes beyond implementing your first wave of rituals. It goes beyond one pass through the Enneagram and a month of meditation and gratitude journaling. Living your calling means continuous and iterative loops through the KNOW-BE-LEAD process. It means periodically checking in on "who am I?" It means stopping every handful of months to see if you feel in alignment with the world around you. It means forming new rituals and continuing to change your life toward sustainable happiness, fulfillment, and, in so doing, reaching fuller potential.

Just as going through KNOW-BE-LEAD this first time was challenging at times, certain parts of subsequent iterations will be as well. Though as you move into greater personal alignment the change will become easier and more natural, enduring change always has elements of difficulty. Your automatic processes and the elephant that supports them never like to go away quietly. In order to avoid transformation resignation and to continue toward your calling for the long term, there are a few closing thoughts we'd like to share with you.

MINDSET REVISITED

As we described in detail at the very beginning of this journey, a growth mindset is our biggest overarching ask of you. Just as it's been important over the course of KNOW-BE-LEAD, it too is important as you try to achieve and sustain the Inside-Out Effect into the future. We hope you are able to channel your growth mindset going forward—we hope you can hold onto its enduring openness and courage to learn and challenge yourself.

Fulfillment is in the journey; it's in every step of progress we make toward the goals we've laid out for ourselves. With a growth mindset, the steps will come easier. Obstacles will be surmountable, criticisms will be digestible, and challenges will be embraceable. As you feel the undertone of the fixed mindset sneak up on you from time to time, opt for the growth mindset. It will serve you better every time.

Not only will striving for a growth mindset help give you the strength and resilience to continue pursuing your calling, it will also affect those you lead. A core part of Dweck's research has shown that leaders who cultivate a growth mindset for both themselves and their teams experience higher rates of innovation. They foster creative workplaces where it's okay to take on a reasonable amount of risk, where it's okay to put your neck on the line, where it's okay to fail. When you lead with a growth mindset, you present skills as learnable and you encourage learning from failure. Solidifying a growth mindset and bringing it to your team, organization, or family will have lasting empowering and positive effects. It will help cement you as a transformational leader.

CELEBRATE!

One of the most important components of successfully continuing to revisit your self-awareness, core values, transformation goals, and rituals is taking the time to celebrate your progress. When you celebrate your wins along the way, it is an acknowledgment of a job well done and is a crucial part of energy management. When you celebrate, do it in the presence of those who have supported you or been a part of the transformation effort. Take your partner out to dinner, go to ice cream with your children, or throw a party with your colleagues. And have fun! When you celebrate, recognize what you've achieved. Show gratitude for those who have helped you. Make it mean something. Just as your C-V Statement and rituals resonate with both your elephant and rider, set up your celebration to do the same.

An incredible real-world example of such a celebratory moment comes from the former Head of the Institute for Healthcare Improvement, Don Berwick.[1] In December 2004, Don gave a speech at a large health care conference. He and his organization had devised a plan to help save the lives of thousands of hospital patients across the country through relatively simple changes to a number of basic hospital procedures. He said, "Here is what I think we should do. I think we should save 100,000 lives. And I think we should do that by June 14, 2006—18 months from today. Some is not a number; soon is not a time. Here's the number: 100,000. Here's the time: June 14, 2006—9 am."

In the months that followed, he and his team worked tirelessly with over 1,000 hospitals to slowly integrate the necessary changes into their day-to-day practices. After a year-and-a-half of incredibly tactful transformation work, there was another industry-wide conference. At 9 am, Don stepped onto the stage and formally acknowledged a time to celebrate.

Hospitals enrolled in the 100,000 Lives Campaign have collectively prevented an estimated 122,300 avoidable deaths and, as importantly, have begun to institutionalize new standards of care that will continue to save lives and improve health outcomes into the future. . . . And, we will celebrate. Starting with pizza and ending with champagne. . . . We will celebrate ourselves because the patients whose lives we save cannot join us, because their names can never be known. Our contribution will be what did not happen to them. And, though they are unknown, we will know that mothers and fathers are at graduations and weddings they would have missed, and that grandchildren will know grandparents they might never have known, and holidays will be taken, and work completed, and books read, and symphonies heard, and gardens tended that, without our work, would have been only beds of weeds.

Don's words opened the floodgates to a perfect celebration. He was both poignant and excited. He was passionate and congratulatory. As you begin to live more and more in line with your calling, we encourage you to celebrate in the same way. Acknowledge where you've been and where you are now. Tie it to the deep meaning within. Remind yourself and your elephant why it is such an incredible and important step in the right direction—the direction of greater fulfillment and performance.

BACK TO THE BEGINNING

When we set out on this journey together, we said that this book was about helping you define "it" on your own terms. Through the nuances of KNOW-BE-LEAD, we've given you the tools to successfully do so. We've shown how performance is intrinsically linked to your happiness and how you can methodically build more fulfillment into your life by working from the inside-out.

As we get ready to part ways for now, we'd like to leave you with a few words from former Presidential Cabinet member and well-known Stanford leadership professor John Gardner.[2] Though

John passed away in 2002, his words are as pertinent today as they were when he first spoke them. The following excerpts are from a speech titled "Personal Renewal" that he gave to a group of young employees at McKinsey & Company near the end of his life. His words are beautifully crafted, and they embody the core tenets of what this book is all about. They continually move and inspire us on our quest to live inside-out.

I said in my book, "Self-Renewal," that we build our own prisons and serve as our own jail-keepers. I no longer completely agree with that. I still think we're our own jailkeepers, but I've concluded that our parents and the society at large have a hand in building our prisons. They create roles for us—and self images—that hold us captive for a long time. The individual intent on self-renewal will have to deal with ghosts of the past—the memory of earlier failures, the remnants of childhood dramas and rebellions, accumulated grievances and resentments that have long outlived their cause. Sometimes people cling to the ghosts with something almost approaching pleasure—but the hampering effect on growth is inescapable. As Jim Whitaker, who climbed Mount Everest, said "You never conquer the mountain, You only conquer yourself" . . .

We want to believe that there is a point at which we can feel that we have arrived. We want a scoring system that tells us when we've piled up enough points to count ourselves successful.

So you scramble and sweat and climb to reach what you thought was the goal. When you get to the top you stand up and look around and chances are you feel a little empty. Maybe more than a little empty.

You wonder whether you climbed the wrong mountain.

But life isn't a mountain that has a summit, Nor is it—as some suppose—a riddle that has an answer. Nor a game that has a final score.

Life is an endless unfolding, and if we wish it to be, an endless process of self-discovery, an endless and unpredictable dialogue between our own potentialities and the life situations in which we find ourselves. By potentialities I mean not just intellectual gifts but the full range of one's capacities for learning, sensing, wondering, understanding, loving and aspiring . . .

After sharing his wisdom with a crowded room of consultants for the better part of a half-hour, Gardner concluded his speech by quoting from an earlier speech he had given on the meaning of life. This is what he said:

Meaning is not something you stumble across, like the answer to a riddle or the prize in a treasure hunt. Meaning is something you build into your life. You build it out of your own past, out of your affections and loyalties, out of the experience of humankind as it is passed on to you, out of your own talent and understanding, out of the things you believe in, out of the things and people you love, out of the values for which you are willing to sacrifice something. The ingredients are there. You are the only one who can put them together into that unique pattern that will be your life. Let it be a life that has dignity and meaning for you. If it does, then the particular balance of success or failure is of less account.

As you pursue your transformation in the weeks and months ahead, may these words guide you as they continually guide us. Remember that life is not a mountain to be summited but is rather an iterative unfolding. It is a malleable journey and only you can lead the way.

ACKNOWLEDGMENTS

The preceding pages would not have been possible without the amazing contributions of countless others.

First and foremost, we'd like to thank several people who truly shaped this work start to finish. Thank you to Avantika Agarwal for her tremendous help with all of our design work. Her tireless attitude and astute eye kept us moving toward a finished product we could be proud of. We are also so grateful for Andrew Bellay and his consistent feedback and content suggestions. He understands the reader experience in a way few do and we are so thankful to have had his perspective with us throughout this whole journey.

Thank you to Tommy Mina, Dominique Fredregill, Will Seaton, Andrew Terrell, Bonnie Chan, Ben Henretig, Dong-Nghi Huynh, Xochitl Watts, and David Corcoran for reading and helping enhance the book as it came along. Your contributions helped us see blind spots we might otherwise have missed.

To all those who joined us in countless high-level discussions about this book's content, thank you. We especially appreciate Leslie Crowell for spending hours of her time helping us frame this book in its early stages, as well as lending us her Enneagram expertise. Her thoughtfulness was indispensable. As well, thank you to Glenn Terrell, Jackie Del Castillo, and Sheila, Nazanin, and Shahin Tabrizi. You pushed back on us when we needed it and spurred us onward when we struggled. We wouldn't have made it without you.

We'd like to thank Melina Uncapher, a research associate at the Stanford Memory Laboratory, for the time and knowledge she shared with us as we began crafting our Brain Bites. Her insight and perspective provided us with an invaluable starting point.

To all of the students in Behnam's *Organizational Change* class at Stanford, thank you for leaving your mark on our lives as well as on these pages. Special thanks to Alex Avery, Andrew LaForge, David DeCastro, Harrison Ward, Patrick Hayes, Samora Garling, Dylan Kordic, and Andrew Chang for helping compile the profiles of several of the famous faces we discussed in the book. We are so grateful for those who shared their stories with us and allowed us, in turn, to share them with you. Specifically, thanks to Leonard Lane and his grandson Alexander Todd Hazen for pulling Leonard's story together at a moment's notice. Thank you to Jeff Smith and Chris Ferry for sharing their stories with us as well.

We appreciate the support and inspiration we received throughout this process from Victor Fung, John Hagel, Justine Musk, and Bethany Nagy.

To our families and close friends, thank you for your ever-present support and love. We truly felt it along the way.

Finally, thank you to you, the reader, for allowing us to share in a powerful moment in your life. May the relationship we've started through the text on these pages find a way to grow as we head off into the future.

NOTES

PREFACE

1. From Bronnie Ware's website: http://www.inspirationandchai.com/Regrets-of-the-Dying.html (accessed June 4, 2012).

INTRODUCTION

1. I Can't Get No ... Job Satisfaction, That Is. (January 2010). *The Conference Board Research Group*. You can find the report online at: http://www.conference-board.org/publications/publicationdetail.cfm?publicationid=1727

2. Ibid.

3. Seligman, M. E. P. (2002). *Authentic Happiness*. New York: Free Press, p. 117.

4. Loehr, J., & Schwartz, T. (2003). *Power of Full Engagement*. New York: Free Press, p. 137.

5. Calculated based on statistics provided by the U.S. Department of Commerce at http://bea.gov/national/index.htm#gdp (accessed October 2011).

6. Inflation-adjusted median family income has grown by 15% in the last 30 years. Data provided by the Census Bureau at: http://www.census.gov/hhes/www/income/data/historical/families/ (Table F-7, All Races) (accessed October 2011).

7. Easterlin, R., McVey, L., Switek, M., Sawangfa, O., & Zweig, J. (2010). The happiness-income paradox revisited. *Proceedings of the National Academy of Sciences, USA*, 107(52), 22463–22468.

8. For a great TED talk on the power of "Why?" see Simon Sinek's speech titled "How Great Leaders Inspire Action": http://www.ted.com/talks/simon_sinek_how_great_leaders_inspire_action.html

9. Ben-Shahar, T. (2007). *Happier*. New York: McGraw-Hill, p. 102. Wrzesniewski's Research: Wrzesniewski, A., & Dutton, J. (2001). Crafting a job: Revisioning employees as active crafters of their work. *Academy of Management Journal*, 26(2), pp. 179–201.

10. Lyubomirsky, S., King, L., & Diener, E. (2005). The benefits of frequent positive effect: Does happiness lead to success? *Psychological Bulletin* 131(6): 803–855.

11. Based on Martin Seligman's work with MetLife Insurance sales agents. See: Seligman, M.E.P. (1991). *Learned Optimism*. New York: Knopf, pp. 97–106.

12. Achor, S. (2010). *The Happiness Advantage*. New York: Crown Business, p. 58.

13. Lyubomirsky, S., King, L., & Diener, E. (2005). The benefits of frequent positive effect: Does happiness lead to success? *Psychological Bulletin* 131(6): 803–855.

14. Direct quote is from Shawn Achor's promotional video for his book *The Happiness Advantage*, link: http://www.youtube.com/watch?v=5rql1tFwMiQ&nore direct=1. He has a similar quote in his TED Talk: "The Happy Secret to Better Work," link: http://www.ted.com/talks/shawn_achor_the_happy_secret_to_better_work.html. Based on his over 10 years of positive psychology research.

15. See research done by psychologist K. Anders Ericsson and his colleagues. Notably: Ericsson, K. A., Krampe, R., & Tesch-Römer, C. (1993). The role of deliberate practice in the acquisition of expert performance. *Psychological Review*, 100(3), pp. 363–406. Also, neurologist Daniel Levitin showcases that 10,000 hours is needed for mastery in numerous fields/pursuits in his book *This Is Your Brain on Music*. See: Levitin, D. (2006). *This Is Your Brain on Music: The Science of a Human Obsession*. New York: Dutton, p. 197.

16. Gladwell, M. (2008). *Outliers: The Story of Success*. New York: Little, Brown and Company, Ch. 2: "The 10,000-Hour Rule."

17. Dweck, C. (2006). *Mindset: The New Psychology of Success*. New York: Ballantine Books.

18. Adapted from Carol Dweck's website: http://mindsetonline.com/changeyour mindset/firststeps/index.html (accessed April 2012).

19. Dweck, *Mindset*, p. 215.

CHAPTER 1: BEGIN THE SEARCH, AVOID THE PITFALLS

1. Heath, C., & Heath, D. (2010) *Switch: How to Change Things When Change Is Hard*. New York: Broadway Books, p. 15.

2. We were first introduced to the concept of not being your story in Landmark Education's "Introduction to Landmark Forum."

3. Mandela, Nelson. (1995). *Long Walk to Freedom: The Autobiography of Nelson Mandela*. New York: Hachette Book Group, p. 286.

4. Spoken by Mandela upon his release from prison on February 11, 1990. For a transcript of his speech, see: http://db.nelsonmandela.org/speeches/pub_view.asp?pg=item&ItemID=NMS016&txtstr

5. Schacter D. L., & Addis, D. R. (2007). The cognitive neuroscience of constructive memory: Remembering the past and imagining the future. *Philosophical Transactions of the Royal Society B*, 362, 773–786.

6. Bransford J., & Johnson, M. K. (1972). Contextual prerequisites for understanding: Some investigations of comprehension and recall. *Journal of Verbal Learning and Verbal Behavior*, 11, 717–726. Neisser, U., editor. (1982). *Memory Observed: Remembering in Natural Contexts*. San Francisco: W.H. Freeman.

7. "I Have a Dream" speech by Martin Luther King Jr.

8. Negativity bias is the name for the psychological phenomenon that explains that humans pay more attention to negative events and thoughts than they do positive or neutral. It's one of the things often cited to explain the propensity of negative news bias. The negative "sells"—or at least holds our attention. For more information, see the seminal paper on the subject by Roy Baumeister and Ellen Bratslavsky: Baumeister, R., Bratslavsky, E., Finkenauer, C., & Vohs, K. (2001). Bad is stronger than good. *Review of General Psychology*, 5(4), 323–370.

9. Soon, C. S., Brass, M., Heinze, H. J., & Haynes, J. D. (2008). Unconscious determinants of free decisions in the human brain. *Nature Neuroscience*, 11, 543–545.

10. Wilson, T. (2004). *Strangers to Ourselves: Discovering the Adaptive Unconscious*. Cambridge, MA: Belknap Press of Harvard University Press, p. 27.

11. Tolle, E. (2005). *A New Earth*. New York: Penguin Group, p. 13.

12. Ibid., p. 27.

13. Based on the traditional characteristics ascribed to the left and right brain.

14. TED talk: "The Divided Brain" by Iain McGilchrist: http://www.ted.com/talks/iain_mcgilchrist_the_divided_brain.html

CHAPTER 2: EXPLORING YOU

1. Type names are based on the Enneagram as it appears in the work of Don Riso and Russ Hudson.

2. Table constructed based on the work of long-time Enneagram student and researcher, Leslie Crowell. Leslie is the Deputy County Executive for Santa Clara

County and is a frequent guest-lecturer on the Enneagram in Behnam's course at Stanford.

3. Riso's and Hudson's QUEST handout. Available online at: http://www.enneagram institute.com/QuestTest.pdf Copyright 2012. The Enneagram Institute. All Rights Reserved. Used with Permission.

4. Myers, I. B., & Myers, P. B. (1995). *Gifts Differing: Understanding Personality Type*. Mountain View, CA: Davies-Black Publishing, "Preface."

5. In the late 1990s, Tom Flautt and John Richards did research in conjunction with the Association of Psychological Type comparing the MBTI to the Enneagram. For more information, see: Flautt, T. (1998) MBTI—Enneagram Type Correlation Study Results. *APT Bulletin of Psychological Type*, 21(8). Also see: http://www.breakoutofthebox.com/flauttrichards.htm (accessed March 2012).

6. Ibid.

7. Madson, P. R. (2005) *Improv Wisdom*. New York: Bell Tower, p. 32.

8. Jobs, S. (2005). Stanford Commencement Address.

9. Emmons, R., & McCullough, M. (2003). Counting blessings versus burdens: An experimental investigation of gratitude and subjective well-being in daily life. *Journal of Personality and Social Psychology*, 84(2), 377–389.

10. Emmons, R. (2008). *Thanks! How Practicing Gratitude Can Make You Happier*. New York: Houghton Mifflin, p. 33.

11. For more information on PQ Reps, check out Shirzad's book: Chamine, S. (2012). *Positive Intelligence*. Austin, TX: Greenleaf Book Group Press, "Chapter 7: PQ Brain Fitness Techniques."

12. Schneider, R. et al. (2005). A randomized controlled trial of stress reduction in African Americans treated for hypertension for over one year. *American Journal of Hypertension*, 18(1), 88–98.

13. Sudsuang, R., Chentanez, V., & Veluvan, K. (1991). Effect of Buddhist mediation on serum cortisol and total protein levels, blood pressure, pulse rate, lung volume, and reaction time. *Physiology & Behavior*, 50(3), 543–548. Barnes, V. A., Davis, H. C., Murzynowski, J. B., & Treiber, F. A. (2004). Impact of mediation on resting and ambulatory blood pressure and heart rate in youth. *Psychosomatic Medicine*, 66(6), 909–914.

14. Solberg, E., Halvorsen, R., Sundgot-Borgen, J., Ingjer, F., & Holen, A. (1995). Mediation: A modulator of the immune response to physical stress? A brief report. *British Journal of Sports Medicine*, 29(4), 255–257.

15. Hölzel, B. K. et al. (2011). Mindfulness practice leads to increases in regional brain gray matter density. *Psychiatry Research: Neuroimaging,* 191(1), 36–43.

16. The Johari Window has well-documented applications in organizational and leadership development. It is a powerful interpersonal communication model. Michael uses it in the *Interpersonal Dynamics* course he facilitates at the Stanford Business School. For more information, see: Luft, J., & Ingham, H. (1955). The Johari Window, A Graphic Model of Interpersonal Awareness. *Proceedings of the Western Training Laboratory in Group Development.* Los Angeles: UCLA.

17. Based predominately on the Enneagram Institute's "Type 5" description: http://www.enneagraminstitute.com/typefive.asp (accessed January, 2012).

18. Ibid.

CHAPTER 3: VISION DEFINED

1. Tichy, N., & Charan, R. (1989). Speed, simplicity, self-confidence: An interview with Jack Welch. *Harvard Business Review.* http://hbr.org/1989/09/speed-simplicity-self-confidence-an-interview-with-jack-welch/ar/1 (accessed November 2011).

2. Loehr, J., & Schwartz, T. (2003). *Power of Full Engagement.* New York: Free Press, p. 142.

3. Spink, K. (1997). *Mother Teresa: A Complete Authorized Biography.* San Francisco: HarperSanFrancisco, p. 6.

4. Ibid., p. 22.

5. Williams, P. (2002). *The Life and Work of Mother Teresa.* Indianapolis, IN: Alpha, p. 68.

CHAPTER 4: GOAL DISCUSSION

1. Cognitive dissonance is the discomfort we experience when we have conflicting cognitions. It usually results in high levels of stress that we try to resolve or alleviate quickly. The classic example is that of smokers. Regular smokers usually reduce the cognitive dissonance between their desire to smoke and its negative health implications by either convincing themselves that they are exceptions to the mortality odds or by adopting a short-term rather than long-term health value system. For more information on cognitive dissonance, see Leon Festinger's seminal work on the subject: Festinger, L. (1957). *A Theory of Cognitive Dissonance.* Stanford, CA: Stanford University Press.

2. Randy Komisar's story is adapted from a field interview in Bill George's book, *True North*. See: George, B. with Sims, P. (2007) *True North: Discover Your Authentic Leadership*. San Francisco: Jossey-Bass, pp. 78–80.

3. Wrzesniewski, A., & Dutton, J. (2001). Crafting a job: Revisioning employees as active crafters of their work. *Academy of Management Journal*, 26(2), pp. 179–201.

4. Based on the term "Positive Deviance" pioneered at Tufts University by Jerry and Monique Sternin. It refers to solving problems by searching for and replicating things that are going/being done well rather than focusing on what's not working. For more information, see: http://www.positivedeviance.org. Also powerfully described as "bright spots" by Chip and Dan Heath in their book *Switch*.

5. Robinson, K. (2009). *The Element: How Finding Your Passion Changes Everything*. New York: Penguin Group, p. 206.

6. Myers, D. (1992) *The Pursuit of Happiness*. New York: Avon Books, p. 43.

7. Ibid., p. 41.

8. Kahneman, D., Krueger, A., Schkade, D., Schwarz, N., & Stone, A. (2006). Would you be happier if you were richer? A focusing illusion. *Science*, 312(5782), 1908–1910.

9. Adapted from a nyoomble.com interview with Leah Kim. http://www.nyoombl.com/video.php?rm=4d957a208aa52 (accessed June 2012).

CHAPTER 5: GOAL FORMATION

1. Solutions-focused brief therapy was developed by Steve de Shazer and his wife Insoo Kim Berg and their team at The Brief Family Therapy Center in Milwaukee. Their work was built on work done at the Palo Alto Mental Research Institute.

2. We first encountered the Miracle and Exception Questions in Chip and Dan Heath's book *Switch* (Heath, C., & Heath, D. (2010) *Switch: How to Change Things When Change Is Hard*. New York: Broadway Books, pp. 34–41). Beyond their work, the Miracle and Exception Questions are rooted in the fundamental philosophy of SFBT. To learn more about their uses, see: de Shazer, S., Dolan, Y., Korman, H., Trepper, T., McCollum, E., & Berg, I. (2007). *More Than Miracles: The State of the Art of Solutions-Focused Brief Therapy*. New York: Routledge, "Chapter 1: A Brief Overview."

3. Albom, M. (1997). *Tuesdays with Morrie: An Old Man, A Young Man, and Life's Greatest Lesson*. New York: Doubleday, pp. 175–176.

CHAPTER 6: MAKE THE CHANGE

1. Haidt, J. (2006). *Happiness Hypothesis*. New York: Basic Books, p. 4. The elephant-rider metaphor is also used extensively and beautifully in Chip and Dan Heath's *Switch*.

2. The Stanford marshmallow experiment is a highly regarded behavioral psychology experiment. In the decades since it was conducted, it has regularly been covered by media and is constantly referred to as a preeminent work on deferred or delayed gratification. Original study: Mischel, W., Ebbesen, E., & Zeiss, A. (1972). Cognitive and attentional mechanisms in delay of gratification. *Journal of Personality and Social Psychology*, 21(2), 204–218. For a great contemporary article, see http://www.newyorker.com/reporting/2009/05/18/090518fa_fact_lehrer?currentPage=1

3. If you'd like to see an awesome/adorable video of a re-created marshmallow experiment, go to: http://www.youtube.com/watch?v=QX_oy9614HQ

4. Arden, J. (2010). *Rewire Your Brain*. Hoboken, NJ: John Wiley & Sons, Inc., "Chapter 1—Firing the Right Cells Together."

5. Zaffron, S., & Logan, D. (2009). *Three Laws of Performance: Rewriting the Future of Your Organization and Your Life*. San Francisco: Jossey-Bass, pp. 36 and 38.

6. Gail Matthews is a Professor of Psychology at Dominican University of California. Her most recent research on goals can be found at: http://cdn.sidsavara.com/wp-content/uploads/2008/09/researchsummary2.pdf (accessed April 2012).

7. Jobs, S. (2005). Stanford Commencement Address.

8. Marianne's original quote appears in her book *A Return to Love*. Source: Williamson, M. (1992). *A Return to Love: Reflections on the Principles of a Course in Miracles*. New York: HarperCollins, p. 190.

9. LeVan, A. (2009). Seeing is believing: The power of visualization. *Psychology Today*. A great example: Ranganathan, V. K. et al. (2004). From mental power to muscle power—gaining strength by using the mind. *Neuropsychologia*, 42(7), 944–956.

10. In his book, *Brain Rules*, University of Washington Bioengineering Professor John Medina discusses how long-term memory formation relies on deliberate, fixed-space repetitions. Manage your energy and your brain by implementing your rituals with even space in between them. Source: Medina, J. (2008) *Brain Rules*. Seattle: Pear Press, pp. 130–133.

11. Further information on unimodal to multimodal event aggregation. Kandel, E. R., Schwartz, J. H., & Jessell, T. M. editors. (2000) *Principles of Neural Science, Fourth Edition.* McGraw-Hill Companies, Inc., Ch. 19, pp. 353–355.

12. Excerpted from Steve Jobs' 2005 Stanford Commencement address.

13. We synthesized Ney Melo's story from several news sources. Notably: http://articles.moneycentral.msn.com/Investing/CNBC/TVReports/Post911 DealMakersShunWallStreet.aspx and http://vitality.yahoo.com/video-second-act-ney-melo-26504189 as well as Ney's personal webpage: http://www.neymelo.com/bio.html (all accessed November 2011).

14. Dolcos, F., LaBar, K. S., & Cabeza, R. (2004). Interaction between the amygdala and the medial temporal lobe memory system predicts better memory for emotional events. *Neuron,* 42(5), 855–863. Cahill, L., Babinsky, R., Markowitsch, H. J, & McGaugh, J. L. (1995). The amygdala and emotional memory. *Nature,* 377(6547), 295–296.

15. Average habit formation is 66 days. http://psychcentral.com/blog/archives/2009/10/07/need-to-form-a-new-habit-66-days/ (accessed March 2012). Original study: Lally, P., van Jaarsveld, C., Potts, H., & Wardle, J. (2010). How are habits formed: Modelling habit formation in the real world. *European Journal of Social Psychology,* (40)6, 998–1009.

16. Wiese, B. S. (2007). Successful pursuit of personal goals and subjective well-being. In B. R. Little, K. Salmela-Aro, and S. D. Phillips (editors), *Personal Project Pursuit: Goals, Action and Human Flourishing.* Hillsdale, NJ: Lawrence Erlbaum, pp. 301–328.

CHAPTER 7: PAY IT FORWARD

1. George, B. with Sims, P. (2007) *True North: Discover Your Authentic Leadership.* San Francisco: Jossey-Bass, p. xxiii.

2. Goleman, D. (1998). What makes a leader? *Harvard Business Review,* pp. 93–102; quote on p. 94.

3. Ibid., p. 94.

4. Ibid., p. 95.

5. Based on Michael's experience facilitating MBA groups as part of the Stanford Business School's *Interpersonal Dynamics* course. This matrix is adapted from Professor Scott Bristol's Values/Behavior Adaptability Matrix in his write-up titled *The Dynamics of Authentic Influence.* Copyright 2003–2010.

6. Kouzes, J., & Posner, B. (1990). The credibility factor: What followers expect from their leaders. *Management Review*, The American Management Association, pp. 29–33.

7. Ibid., p. 32.

8. Based on the Harvard Business School case prepared by John Kotter titled "Renn Zaphiropoulos." HBS No. 9-480-044. Revised October 14, 1993.

9. Based on the Harvard Business School case prepared by John Kotter titled "Fred Henderson." HBS No. 480-043.

10. Rosenthal, R., & Jacobson, L. (1968). *Pygmalion in the Classroom*. New York: Holt, Rinehart & Winston.

11. Kahn, W. (1990). Psychological conditions of personal engagement and disengagement at work. *Academy of Management Journal*, 33(4), pp. 692–724.

12. Hackman, R., & Oldham, G. (1976). Motivation through the design of work: Test of a theory. *Organizational Behavior and Human Performance*, 16, pp. 250–279.

13. Likert, R. (1961). *New Patterns in Management*. New York: McGraw-Hill.

14. Welch, J. (2005). "It's Not About You" speech at the Stanford Graduate School of Business.

15. Easwaran, Eknath. (1978). *Gandhi the Man*. Berkley: The Blue Mountain Center of Meditation, Inc., p. 12. Most of Gandhi's story is based on this book, pp. 11–38.

16. Ibid., p. 17.

17. Ibid., p. 21.

18. Ibid., p. 29.

19. Ibid., p. 38.

CHAPTER 8: A CONTINUOUS JOURNEY

1. Rao, H., & Hoyt, D. (2008). "Institute for Healthcare Improvement: The Campaign to Save 100,000 Lives." Stanford GSB Case Study L-13. We had the pleasure of first encountering this case in Chip and Dan Heath's book *Switch*.

2. Gardner, J. (1990) Speech titled "Personal Renewal." Delivered to McKinsey & Co. in Phoenix, AZ.

ABOUT THE AUTHORS

Behnam Tabrizi is a leading global business consultant, best-selling author, and award-winning teacher and scholar. He is a Consulting Professor at Stanford University's Department of Management Science and Engineering, and an internationally recognized expert and thought leader on corporate and leadership transformation. He has written five books on managing change and transformation, and as an advisor to many Fortune 500 companies, the U.S. President, and several governmental agencies, he has helped thousands of CEOs and leaders plan, mobilize, and implement transformational initiatives that have elevated organizational performance and created unprecedented results. Dr. Tabrizi's research with McKinsey & Co. on more than 100 companies around the globe on "Accelerating Transformation" was featured in *Forbes*, the *Chicago Tribune*, *The Washington Post*, and the *San Jose Mercury News* as a "pioneering work." He has also been interviewed by the BBC and C-SPAN regarding his recent work on transformation. Dr. Tabrizi has served on the boards of Clever Sense (recently sold to Google) and Catapult Ventures, and has held positions at the Harvard Business School and the Stanford Graduate School of Business. He is the Chairman of Rapid Transformation, LLC based in Palo Alto, California.

To learn more about Behnam's and his team's work,
please visit www.rapidtransformation.com

Michael Terrell is a leader in the personal transformation field and founder of the Terrell Leadership Group—a firm that specializes in helping Silicon Valley leaders develop authentic and effective leadership capabilities that have measurable impacts on their company cultures, business outcomes, relationships, and personal well-being. In addition to his industry work, Michael facilitates learning groups for one of the most popular courses at the Stanford Graduate School of Business called Interpersonal Dynamics, in which he helps students develop awareness and communication skills that cultivate emotional intelligence and will serve them powerfully in their next phases of leadership. Michael has a B.S. in Management Science and Engineering from Stanford University where he was a Mayfield Fellow.

To learn more about Michael and his work,
please visit www.terrellleadership.com